To the Mead Public Library

John H. Schroeder

April, 2015

D1715530

THE BATTLE OF
LAKE CHAMPLAIN

C&C

CAMPAIGNS & COMMANDERS

GREGORY J. W. URWIN, SERIES EDITOR

THE BATTLE OF
LAKE CHAMPLAIN

A "Brilliant and Extraordinary Victory"

JOHN H. SCHROEDER

UNIVERSITY OF OKLAHOMA PRESS | NORMAN

Library of Congress Cataloging-in-Publication Data

Schroeder, John H., 1943–
The Battle of Lake champlain : A "brilliant and extraordinary victory" / John H.
Schroeder.
    pages cm. — (Campaigns and commanders series ; 49)
Includes bibliographical references and index.
ISBN 978-0-8061-4693-5 (hbk. : alk. paper)
    1. Lake Champlain, Battle of, N.Y., 1814. 2. United States—History—War of
1812—Peace. I. Title. II. Title: Battle of Lake Champlain.
    E356.P7S37 2014
    973.5′256—dc23
                            2014030785

The Battle of Lake Champlain: A "Brilliant and Extraordinary Victory" is
Volume 49 in the Campaigns and Commanders series.

The paper in this book meets the guidelines for permanence and durability of the
Committee on Production Guidelines for Book Longevity of the Council on Library
Resources, Inc. ∞

1 2 3 4 5 6 7 8 9 10

Interior layout and composition: Alcorn Publication Design

For Reginald Horsman, an abiding friend and mentor.

Contents

Illustrations

Figures

Maps

Table

Preface

On September 11, 1814, on Lake Champlain, an American naval squadron under Master Commandant Thomas Macdonough decisively defeated a formidable British force under the command of Captain George Downie.[1] The battle was fiercely fought and closely contested. During the two-and-one-half hour struggle, momentum shifted on several occasions as one side and then the other gained the upper hand. When the last of the British warships surrendered, Governor in Chief Sir George Prevost, the senior civilian and military official for British North America, ordered the immediate retreat of his invading army in nearby Plattsburgh, New York, even though it was on the verge of routing the greatly outnumbered American defenders of the village. This dramatic victory gave the Americans total naval control of the lake and ended the invasion of the Champlain Valley. Within three days, all 10,000 British troops of the invasion force had marched back across the border into Canada.

Historians have long considered the Battle of Lake Champlain a critical event in the War of 1812. In addition to its immediate military effect, the battle had far-reaching consequences in Canada, the United States, London, and Ghent, in the Netherlands, where peace talks were underway. Secretary of Navy William Jones labeled it soon afterward a "brilliant and extraordinary victory" and a "splendid and memorable event." Historians have often used the word "decisive" to describe the battle. "More nearly than any other incident of the War of 1812," wrote Captain Alfred Thayer Mahan in *Sea Power in Its Relations to the War of 1812*, "the Battle of Lake Champlain merits the epithet 'decisive.'" In *The Naval War of 1812*, Theodore Roosevelt labeled Macdonough the "greatest figure in our naval history" for his victory "against decided odds in ships, men and metal." David G. Fitz-Enz simply titled his book *The Final Invasion: Plattsburgh, the War of 1812's Most Decisive Battle*. Winston Churchill called it simply "the most decisive engagement of the war" in his monumental *History of the English-Speaking People*. Although most historians concur with this general assessment, some disagree. With respect to Plattsburgh and Lake Champlain, Jon Latimer in his *1812: War against America* denied that it was the most decisive engagement. "Plattsburgh helped to convince the British to come to terms but had little wider significance." Other historians, such as Troy Bickham in *The Weight of Vengeance: The United States, the British Empire, and the War of 1812,* have deemphasized the events on Lake Champlain and around Plattsburgh by stressing international factors. Although some historians continue to quibble over exactly how decisive the battle was, I did not want to engage that debate.

My purpose in writing this book was threefold. First, I wanted to place the dramatic events on Lake Champlain and in Plattsburgh in the context of the larger war between the United States and Great Britain in North America. Lake Champlain and the surrounding valley stood historically as the key section of the historic Great Warpath, which stretched from Ticonderoga and Lake George, New York, north to Montreal and Quebec in Lower Canada. This strategic corridor offered the most direct and accessible invasion route north or south between the Hudson River Valley and Lower Canada. For decades, the Great Warpath had been a critical and hotly contested territory in conflicts for control of the region. An important question, then, was not why did Lake Champlain became the site of such an important battle, but rather why did it take more than two long years for that event to occur?

Second, I wanted to explain how and why the Americans achieved their unlikely and unexpected victory on Lake Champlain and in Plattsburgh. Macdonough's victory and Prevost's precipitous withdrawal came as a great surprise in Canada, the United States, and Great Britain. After all, how could an unseasoned thirty-year-old American officer devastate a formidable British flotilla commanded by a seasoned naval captain? Moreover, how could a small American army force into retreat a much larger British army that included many seasoned veterans from Europe? In fact, the U.S. victory resulted from a combination of small and large factors that determined the outcome. Preparation and planning, individual valor and cowardice, brilliant and poor command decisions, and just plain good and bad luck all played an important role.

Third, I sought to explain fully the extensive political and diplomatic results of the events on Lake Champlain and in Plattsburgh. In his classic study *The Era of Good Feelings,* George Dangerfield wrote, "When *Confiance* struck her colors to the *Saratoga* in Plattsburgh Bay on September 11, the effect was felt from Canada to Vienna." In this book I have attempted to describe these various effects in Canada, the United States, London, and Ghent.

I had the special privilege to spend the 2010–11 academic year as the Class of 1957 Distinguished Professor of American Naval Heritage at the U.S. Naval Academy. During that year, I was encouraged by Professors Craig Symonds and Fred Harrod as well as other colleagues to write a book about the American navy's role in the War of 1812 and specifically the Battle of Lake Champlain. I was familiar with this dramatic action and its military importance, but I did not fully understand its far-reaching repercussions. As I began to study it closely, I realized that an opportunity existed to write a book that placed the battle in its larger context in the War of 1812 and explained its true significance. I quickly came to realize that it was, indeed, a pivotal and underappreciated moment in American history.

Once I finished the manuscript, I relied on Reginald Horsman and James Bradford to read and critique it. As they had done with other books I had written, they furnished insightful comments and numerous suggestions that significantly improved the final version. As always, I am indebted to them. John Grodzinski's comments clarified several key points about the British invasion of New York and saved me from a number of factual errors. At the University of Oklahoma Press, the efforts of Stephanie Attia, Anna María Rodríguez, and Tom Jonas helped greatly in the production process. The manuscript was strengthened by the thorough and meticulous work of copyeditor Kevin Brock. As she has been with all of my other books, my wife, Sandra, was my toughest and my best critic. Over countless hours that she could have better spent in her garden or with her friends, she improved the clarity and precision of the narrative while excising typos, stylistic gremlins, and grammatical mistakes.

Note: Although both the names Cumberland Bay and Plattsburgh Bay are used in some histories, I have used Cumberland Bay for consistency.

THE BATTLE OF
LAKE CHAMPLAIN

PROLOGUE

The British squadron came into full view as it rounded Cumberland Head shortly after eight o'clock on September 11, 1814. The battle was at hand. After days of intermittent wet weather, this Sunday brought a bright sunny morning on Lake Champlain. A brisk breeze from the northeast had carried the British ships quickly up the lake. This force consisted of four fighting ships, ten gunboats, and two support vessels. Dominating the scene was the largest warship ever to sail the lake, the 37-gun frigate HMS *Confiance.* On board stood the British commander, Captain George Downie, a supremely confident and seasoned officer who was determined to destroy the American enemy.

Awaiting the British in Plattsburgh Bay were four American warships, which rested quietly at anchor. Close by were ten gunboats. Their commander, thirty-year-old Master Commandant Thomas Macdonough, surveyed the enemy from the deck of the 26-gun *Saratoga.* Macdonough was a talented, promising, but yet unproven officer who had never commanded a warship, much less a squadron, in actual combat.

On shore in Plattsburgh, a British army stood poised to overwhelm its American enemies. There, north of the Saranac River, which divided the village, more than 8,000 British troops waited for the command to attack. This force included more than 2,600 veterans from the Duke of Wellington's army. Having fought victoriously in Spain, they had been sent to Canada to spearhead an invasion of the United States. The senior British commander, Sir George Prevost, was the governor in chief of Canada and had served in the army for thirty-five years. Prevost had an indifferent record as a field commander, but the British would actually be led into battle by three of Wellington's finest major generals.

Entrenched in three small forts and two blockhouses across the Saranac River in Plattsburgh was an American force of less than 1,800 regulars who had been supplemented by the recent arrival of several hundred militia volunteers. Brigadier General Alexander Macomb commanded the outnumbered Americans. Trained as an engineer and artillery officer, the thirty-two-year-old Macomb was a capable officer but had little combat experience and had never commanded a large army in battle. In fact, up until just two weeks before, he had been only second in command of the American army in the area, taking charge only when Major General George Izard departed in late August for western New York. Izard took with him most of the troops who had been stationed near the Lake Champlain border.

Although Prevost's ultimate objective was secret, some Americans assumed that he intended to do what British general John Burgoyne had tried and failed to do during the American Revolution: that is, to march south along Lake Champlain, capture Saratoga and Fort Ticonderoga, and then continue south to the Hudson River Valley and Albany. At stake on September 11, then, was considerably more than naval control of Lake Champlain or the military possession of Plattsburgh. Even if the British chose not to advance beyond Plattsburgh, their expected military victory would give them control of the lake and possession of northern New York, placing British diplomats in a strong position to demand territorial concessions from the United States as a condition of peace.

The timing of the battle made September 11, 1814, the pivotal moment in the War of 1812. The first two years of the conflict had been indecisive in North America. Numerous U.S. attempts to invade Canada had failed, but the British had never seriously threatened the American homeland. Then in 1814, after France and Napoleon had been defeated in early April, the war took a dangerous turn for the United States. Now free to give the Americans a good "drubbing," the British dramatically escalated their war effort. They extended and tightened their blockade of the American coast while sending thousands of veteran troops to Canada to attack U.S. territory. British forces attacked and occupied the coast of Maine while a large diversionary armada sailed to Chesapeake Bay. Another invasion was planned for New Orleans and the Gulf coast. A perceptive Maryland politician noted that the United States would now have to fight "not for free Trade and sailors rights, not for the Conquest of the Canadas, but for our national Existence."

This prediction proved prescient during the summer of 1814. The British tightened their blockade and raided New England coastal towns. In mid-August the large armada sailed unopposed up Chesapeake Bay, its land contingent capturing and burning Washington, D.C., on August 24. Several days later Alexandria, Virginia, capitulated without resistance to another British force. As panic and uncertainty spread, alarmed officials in Philadelphia and New York scrambled to raise troops for local defense. By September 10, the armada in the Chesapeake stood poised to assault Baltimore. Meanwhile, Nantucket Island had declared its neutrality and left the war. In Maine British forces soon controlled one hundred miles of the coast from Hampden to Eastport. From Canada, after more than 12,000 reinforcements had arrived, one British army invaded New York and occupied Plattsburgh on Lake Champlain, while another was expected to attack Sackets Harbor, New York, on Lake Ontario.

The condition of Washington, D.C., added to the disheartening situation. The capital itself lay in shambles. The British had burned the Executive Mansion and the Capitol, which also housed the Library of Congress. They had also destroyed the Treasury building and the offices of the War and State Departments. The Navy Yard had also been burned. The only government agency spared damage was the Patent Office. A number of private buildings and homes had also been destroyed. In the days after the British left, looters roamed Washington and graffiti soon defaced the walls of the Capitol.

The nation's government was also in disarray. President James Madison inspired little confidence. In addition to the secretary of war, who had resigned in disgrace, the cabinet was without a treasury secretary and would soon be without a naval secretary. Congress was about to convene and learn that the nation urgently needed to raise thousands of additional troops. But recruitment lagged while desertions had risen sharply in recent months. Moreover, the nation faced a desperate financial situation. Close to running out of money, the government could barely pay its most pressing military bills. "Something must be done and speedily," observed naval secretary William Jones, "or we shall have an opportunity of trying the experiment of maintaining an army and navy and carrying on a vigorous war without money."

Political criticism of the president and the war had also sharpened. "Without money, without soldiers & without courage," declared New York Federalist senator Rufus King, "the President and his Cabinet are the objects of general execration." In New England, opposition to the war had always been strong, but now it intensified. In Boston the situation was particularly tense as all of this disturbing news poured into the city. In addition, against only light resistance, the British had taken formal possession of eastern Maine, bottling up the 28-gun *Adams* in the Penobscot River and forcing its commander to burn the ship. Many expected an attack on Boston to be next. A contentious town meeting there demanded action to defend the city. Massachusetts governor Caleb Strong first called out the militia on September 4, then called a special session of the legislature for early October to discuss holding a special convention of New England states to register their grievances with the federal government and possibly consider secession from the Union. On September 10 the *Boston Centinel* proclaimed that the "Union was already practically dissolved, and that the people must rise in their majesty, protect themselves and compel their unworthy servants to obey their will." There were even disturbing rumors of a separate peace between New England and the enemy.

On September 11 the critical moment had come. That morning in northern New York, only Macdonough's anchored ships in Plattsburgh Bay and Macomb's outnumbered men in the town of Plattsburgh stood between the British and disaster for the United States.

CHAPTER I

THE INDECISIVE NORTHERN
THEATER, 1812 AND 1813

It had taken more than two improbable and inconclusive years of fighting to reach this pivotal moment on Lake Champlain. When the war began in June 1812, many Americans predicted confidently that a quick and decisive invasion of Canada would end the war by forcing British concessions to their grievances. They also expected the invasion would be an easy undertaking. Before the war, from the comfortable isolation of Monticello, Thomas Jefferson had written that taking Canada was "a mere matter of marching." Likewise, Speaker of the House Henry Clay, a "War Hawk" in Congress, predicted that "the militia of Kentucky are alone competent to place Montreal and Upper Canada at our feet."[1]

Vocal support also existed for the permanent acquisition of Canada. Jefferson wrote of the invasion as preparation for "the final expulsion of England from the American continent." Representative R. M. Johnson of Kentucky declared that because of Great Britain's "deadly and implacable enmity, and her continued hostilities, I shall never die contented until I see her expulsion from North America, and her territories incorporated with the United States." Many in the West strongly agreed with Johnson. Given the popular support for annexation, Secretary of State James Monroe acknowledged that it would be "difficult to relinquish Territory which had been conquered."[2]

Most U.S. leaders, however, viewed the invasion of Canada only as a military strategy, not as a prelude to annexation. Despite his misgivings, Monroe predicted, "In the case of war, it might be necessary to invade Canada: not as an object of the war, but as a means of bring[ing] it to a satisfactory conclusion." Once hostilities began, Speaker Clay stated that Canada "is not the end but the means, the object of the War being the redress of injuries, and Canada being the instrument by which that redress was to be obtained." In other words, a successful invasion would force Britain to accept peace on U.S. terms, bringing an end to the practice of impressment and other violations of American neutral rights on the seas.[3]

Although it had seemed entirely reasonable when the fighting began, American confidence soon proved to be badly misplaced. Americans acknowledged that on paper Great Britain had over-whelming military and economic superiority but believed that two factors would offset those advantages. First, Britain was tied down by its war with Napoleon in Europe. North America would be a secondary military theater to which it could not send additional ground and naval forces. Second, the actual fighting would occur in North America, where the British colonies included Lower and Upper Canada, Nova Scotia, and New Brunswick. Canada appeared to be very vulnerable because its lightly defended border stretched about 1,000 miles from Quebec to the Detroit frontier at the western tip of Lake Erie.[4]

In June 1812 the United States also appeared to be in a formidable military position to overwhelm Canada. Its population numbered approximately 7.5 million compared to Canada's 500,000 residents. The 6,000-man U.S. Army was roughly the same size as British forces in Canada, but the United States expected to increase the size of its fighting force much more rapidly than the enemy could. Presumably, state militias could be called up and volunteers would rush to arms. In contrast, London surely had no intention of sending reinforcements to North America from Europe, where Britain's best officers and soldiers were already fighting. In addition, in both Lower and Upper Canada, government officials worried about the loyalty of its residents and militia units. In Lower Canada more than two-thirds of the population were French Canadians who felt little loyalty, and in some cases considerable antipathy, toward their British rulers. In sparsely settled Upper Canada, an estimated one-third of residents were recent settlers who had migrated from the United States. There, as the war began, British major general Isaac Brock labeled most of the people "either indifferent to what is passing, or so completely American as to rejoice in the prospects of a change of Governments." New York governor Daniel Tompkins confidently estimated that one-half of the Canadian militia would "join our standard" once an invasion began.[5]

Critical to American confidence and military expectations was the geography of Canada. Likened at the time to a large tree, Canada's

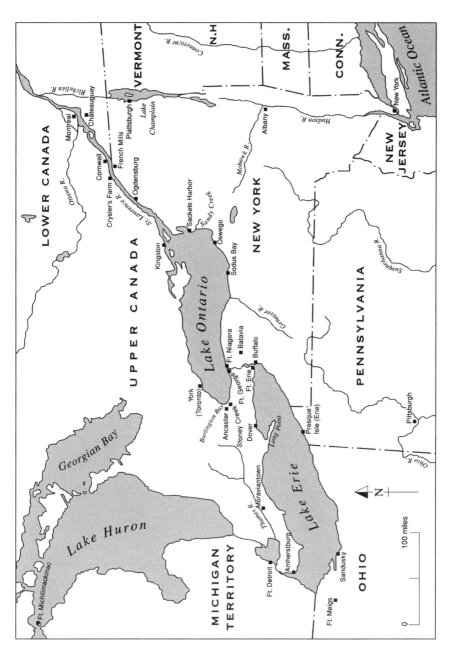

The Northern Theater of War. From Grodzinski, *Defender of Canada*, 204. Used by permission of Robin Brass Studio, Inc.

roots stretched into the Atlantic Ocean, with its trunk being the Saint Lawrence River and its branches extending far westward into Lake Ontario, Lake Erie, Lake Huron, and beyond. Its mainland consisted of two parts. Lower Canada included the major settlements of Quebec and Montreal and extended to the Ottawa River west of Montreal. Upper Canada stretched to the west through the Great Lakes and included small settlements along their northern shores.

The key strategic points were identified as Quebec and Montreal in Lower Canada, while a few in Upper Canada were deemed important but of lesser significance, namely Kingston on eastern Lake Ontario, the Niagara frontier between Lakes Ontario and Erie, and the Detroit frontier on the western edge of Lake Erie. Far to the west were tiny U.S. outposts at Fort Mackinac and Fort Dearborn (later Chicago). Located near the mouth of the Saint Lawrence River, Quebec was the largest and most important settlement but well protected by British naval forces based nearby in Halifax. Montreal, then, stood as the primary American military objective because its position on the Saint Lawrence commanded the only supply and communication line between Lower and Upper Canada. The city was vulnerable to invasion either down the river from Lake Ontario or from Lake Champlain in nearby New York.

Since the United States did not control Lake Ontario or the upper Saint Lawrence, the most direct route to Montreal would be north from Lake Champlain, across the border, and down the Richelieu River to the Saint Lawrence just north of the city.[6] Lake Champlain stood at the center of this military corridor stretching roughly 200 miles from Albany, New York, to Montreal. To the north, Lake Champlain flows into the Richelieu, which empties into the Saint Lawrence at Sorrel, seventy-five miles from Montreal. Near the southern end of Lake Champlain, a small tongue of land several miles long separates it from Lake George. From the southern end of either lake, it is only twenty miles by one route and thirty by another to Fort Edwards, which was then the northernmost navigable point on the Hudson River and just forty miles north of Albany.

Known as the "Great Warpath," this corridor already had a long and rich military history by 1812. In the century after its European discovery by Samuel de Champlain in 1609, colonial interest in the valley lagged, and it remained virtually unsettled by whites. Then, during the four imperial wars between Britain and France from 1689 to 1763, the Champlain Valley became an occasional point of conflict

THE INDECISIVE NORTHERN THEATER 11

between the two powers and their Indian allies. Before 1754, the valley remained largely unsettled, but the French built forts at Crown Point and Carillon (later Ticonderoga) to assert their control. During the French-Indian War (or Seven Years' War, 1756–63), the valley became a point of heated contention. The British took Fort Carillon and Crown Point and then built a military road from Crown Point across the Green Mountains to the Connecticut Valley. In 1760 the capture of Montreal placed the region firmly under British control. The treaty that ended the war in 1763 gave Great Britain permanent control of Lake Champlain.

After 1763 the population of the region grew slowly, but the Champlain-Richelieu corridor played a significant military role during the American Revolution. In 1775 Ethan Allen and the Green Mountain Boys seized the lightly defended British garrisons at Fort Ticonderoga and Crown Point. Then in the fall of 1775, an American force of six hundred men under the command of Major General Richard Montgomery marched north. It captured the British forts at Chambly and Saint John before seizing Montreal in November 1775. From there, Montgomery's force moved down the Saint Lawrence and joined three hundred American militiamen under Colonel Benedict Arnold in an effort to capture Quebec. The attack on December 31 was a disaster, with Montgomery being killed and Arnold seriously wounded. Although they had been repelled, the Americans remained outside the city during the winter before British reinforcements forced them to retreat in the spring of 1776. The Revolution would not officially begin until that July, but the Champlain Valley had already demonstrated its military importance.

In 1776 the British easily retook Montreal and then marched south to Lake Champlain. Under the command of Governor General Sir Guy Carleton, the British intended to take Champlain and key points such as Fort Ticonderoga before continuing south to the Hudson River and Albany, where they expected to meet a British army moving north from New York City. They quickly advanced up the Richelieu River and Champlain to Crown Point, where the force halted in order to build a naval squadron at Saint Johns to take control of the lake. Carleton had the 28-gun *Inflexible* dismantled on the Saint Lawrence, transported to Lake Champlain, and reassembled there. His men also built a 12-gun and a 14-gun schooner, twenty gunboats, a gondola, and a floating battery (radeau) mounting twelve guns. With only four small gunboats in his possession,

American commander Arnold retreated to the south end of the lake at Skenesboro to build his own squadron. During July and August, his men constructed six flat-bottomed vessels carrying three guns each and six galleys carrying eight to ten guns each.[7]

Although he later became the Revolution's most famous traitor, Arnold was nevertheless a resourceful, courageous, inspiring, and brilliant commander who served the American cause with genuine distinction early in the war. When the British began their move south, Arnold positioned his squadron in the lee of Valcour Island along the lake's western shore. On October 11 the British had already sailed past the island before spotting the American vessels. With the wind out of the north, Carleton had to beat back with difficulty to windward to close on Arnold. The Americans fought effectively, but they were overpowered by the superior firepower of the British and were saved only by darkness from complete defeat.

The prevailing wind prevented Arnold's flight to the north while the British blocked escape to the south. He did, however, manage in early morning darkness and fog to slip past the enemy in shallow waters along the shoreline. Once Carleton discovered the American escape, his squadron pursued and eventually destroyed or forced all but five of Arnold's boats to beach themselves. The Battle of Valcour Island was a decisive British victory. Arnold had lost control of Lake Champlain and eleven of his sixteen vessels, but Carleton decided that the time it had taken to win command of the lake made it too late in the campaign season to complete his march southward to the Hudson River. Accordingly, he withdrew his forces to Saint John's for the winter. When the British campaign resumed under General John Burgoyne in the spring of 1777, it faced no opposition on Champlain. But the American army that had been in disarray the previous fall was now in stronger shape. The eventual result was not an easy march to the Hudson but a decisive American victory that October at Saratoga, where Major General Horatio Gates defeated and captured the entire invading British army. When news of this victory reached Europe, it was instrumental in convincing France to sign an alliance with the Continental government. Ironically, Arnold's defeat at Valcour Island in 1776 played a significant role in the victory at Saratoga by delaying the British advance for a year.[8]

Now in 1812, three decades after the Revolution, the Champlain Valley seemed sure to reassume its importance in American military strategy. The war plan was developed by Major General Henry

Dearborn shortly before the war began. The sixty-one-year-old Dearborn had fought with distinction in the Revolutionary War and subsequently served in various capacities before becoming secretary of war under President Jefferson. He then served for several years as Boston's customs collector before President Madison appointed him as one of the nation's two major generals in 1811. Dearborn's plan called for a coordinated, multipronged invasion of Canada.[9] Recognizing that Quebec was inaccessible, the key objective would be Montreal, which would be attacked from a base at Lake Champlain. Coordinated with this main operation would be secondary offensives against Upper Canada, targeting Kingston on Lake Ontario, the Niagara frontier, and the Detroit frontier. Since he expected success, Dearborn did not consider any less ambitious alternatives such as seizing and holding a strong point on the Saint Lawrence River above Montreal. While avoiding an assault on the well-defended town, such a move would have isolated Upper Canada by severing its communication and supply line to Lower Canada. As the U.S. naval commander on Lake Ontario, Commodore Isaac Chauncey, explained later, "The best means to conquer the Canada's [sic] was . . . by maintaining a Position on the St. Lawrence—this would be winning the tree by 'girdling'—the branches deprived of the ordinary Supplies from the root, die of necessity."[10]

Although it seemed logical on paper, the American war plan was not operationally feasible because the Madison administration and Congress had not prepared for war, much less for a multipronged invasion of Canada. Headed by William Eustis, a politician without military expertise, the War Department was staffed only by eight civilian clerks and lacked a chief of staff or a unified command structure; several years earlier, the position of quartermaster general had also been eliminated. As a result, no system existed to supply a large army with provisions, equipment, and ordnance. The primitive state of overland communications along most of the long Canadian border made it virtually impossible to coordinate a complex attack from the United States. Given the mostly untouched wilderness and lack of passable roads along much of the border, the offensives would require waterborne transportation, yet apparently no thought had been given to the issue of naval control of Lakes Ontario and Erie.[11]

The United States also lacked enough capable officers and seasoned soldiers to conduct a coordinated operation. On paper the army had a sufficient number of senior officers, but virtually all of them were Revolutionary War veterans. Unlike the navy, whose officers had seen action in the Quasi-War with France and the Barbary War, most in the army had no recent combat experience. Now in their late fifties and sixties, many of these men had been civilians for decades and were long past their military primes. Nor did the United States have sufficient troops. The regular army consisted of about six thousand troops scattered on posts around the country rather than clustered near the northern border. Volunteers might be raised within several months, but these men were going to be raw, untested, and undisciplined at the outset. A better source of manpower would be the state militias. The best of these were from New England, but it was here that the war was most unpopular. In states like Massachusetts, Connecticut, New York, and Vermont, the militia might be available to defend its home state but not to invade Canada. In fact, New Englanders refused to allow their forces to be controlled by the federal government at all.

The United States had also failed to recognize the quality of British leadership in Canada. As governor in chief, Sir George Prevost was in charge of both the military and the civilian government. Canada was vulnerable and divided between its British minority and its French Canadian majority, but Prevost proved particularly well qualified to deal with these challenges. Not a native-born Englishman, he had been born in the colony of New Jersey in 1767, whose father was a Swiss Protestant career officer in the British military and his mother the daughter of a wealthy Amsterdam banker. He had been educated in Europe as well as in England and spoke French fluently.[12]

Prevost entered the British military at age twelve and rose steadily in rank. He led troops in combat with distinction against French forces on Barbados, Saint Lucia, and Dominica; served as the civilian lieutenant governor on Saint Lucia; and later was governor of Dominica. From 1808 to 1811, Prevost served as lieutenant governor of Nova Scotia with the rank of lieutenant general. In 1809 he served as second in command of an expedition that captured the French colony of Martinique.

In 1811, when he became governor in chief of British North America, the forty-four-year-old Prevost had amassed an impressive military and administrative résumé and had performed well as the conciliatory civilian administrator of Saint Lucia and Dominica.

Upon assuming his new duties, Prevost began to prepare Canada for war with the United States by winning the support of French Canadian political leaders and the Roman Catholic hierarchy, which had been seriously alienated by his predecessor, Governor Sir James Craig. He also received approval to raise two new corps of Canadian troops and appointed Major General Brock to command Upper Canada.

The London government instructed Prevost to prepare a plan to defend Canada but warned that he was not to plan any offensive operations against the United States and emphasized that the war in Europe precluded them from sending additional reinforcements to North America. Intending to defend both Lower and Upper Canada, Prevost's eventual plan was well adapted to his instructions, the size of his forces, the probability of U.S. attacks, and the geography of Canada. It detailed the weaknesses of each British military outpost along the 1,500-mile border from Fort Joseph, on the northwestern end of Lake Huron, to Quebec. With most of its outposts in physical disrepair and manned by only a few British regulars or fencibles, Upper Canada was particularly vulnerable to American attacks. Accordingly, Prevost's defensive strategy considered "the preservation of Quebec as its first object, and to which all others must be subordinate." Since the presence of the Royal Navy made Quebec relatively secure from American assaults, Prevost stressed the defense of Montreal, which he saw as "the first object of Attack." But while planning to concentrate his forces in Lower Canada, he had no intention of abandoning Upper Canada. Sending large numbers of reinforcements was out of the question, but Prevost sought to strengthen defenses there by securing the communications and supply routes on the Saint Lawrence River and Lakes Ontario and Erie. By controlling these critical inland waterways, he would be able to send reinforcements and supplies to Upper Canada without interruption.[13]

Although Prevost did not know the details of the American war plan, he fully expected attacks against both Lower and Upper Canada, with the main offensive to be launched from Lake Champlain against Montreal. As hostilities approached, the governor deployed his forces accordingly. Although the loyalty and discipline of militias in Lower Canada was thought to be suspect, Prevost overcame some initial difficulties to produce a force that was steady and reliable. To protect the southern approach to Montreal, he reinforced the area between Laprairie and Champlain. By the end of July

1812, about 4,000 regulars and militiamen were in place, including 1,600 halfway between Saint-Jean and Laprairie (twenty-seven miles from Champlain), 600 at Lacadie, 500 at Isle-aux-Noix, and others at Saint-Jean and Chambly. Prevost transported several gunboats overland to strengthen the outpost at Isle-aux-Noix and had all the roads leading to the U.S. border blocked.[14]

When war came, the Madison administration was ill prepared to attack Montreal from Lake Champlain. General Dearborn had established his headquarters at Greenbush, New York, across the Hudson River from Albany, a site that furnished him reasonable proximity to American operations on Champlain and in western New York. Dearborn then traveled to New England, where he spent weeks attempting unsuccessfully to recruit volunteers and to persuade states to send their militias west. As a result, the slow trickle of troops congregating near Lake Champlain precluded an early offensive against Montreal.

Although Dearborn was slow to raise troops, he understood the importance of maintaining the loyalty of American Indians in the region and of receiving reliable intelligence from Canada. He needed to know the size of enemy forces, where they were stationed, and what their movements were. Accordingly, Dearborn sought out and convinced Eleazer Williams, who was an itinerant preacher and missionary, to maintain the loyalty of Indians and to furnish this critical intelligence. As Williams put it, "I am sent for to prevent the Indians from taking the hatchet against the Americans."[15]

Born in 1788, Williams was a mixed-blood Caughnawaga who had grown up in a large Indian family on a reservation where his father was an important chief. Educated at a Congregational seminary, he was a bright, energetic, and religious young man of twenty. As a devout Congregationalist with strong pacifist beliefs, he was very reluctant to become involved in a war, but Dearborn met and convinced him to join the American cause. The general agreed to pay him four hundred dollars a year plus two rations per day and expenses for travel. He also gave him the title of superintendent general of the Northern Indian Department and commander of the Corps of Observation. Initially, Williams served under New York militia major general Benjamin Mooers at Plattsburgh. From there, he recruited a group of "rangers" to assist him. Although his antiwar conscience bothered him, Williams and his rangers performed important services. He conferred with and executed missions for all of the American generals in the Lake Champlain area during the war. His rangers became the eyes and ears of the American army in the region: "No movement made by the enemy but is known to them." Williams proudly noted that his "secret corps of observation" was "always in motion and activity, ready to execute the order of the government however delicate and dangerous the nature of it may be. . . . Their courage, bravery and fidelity save them—the war department often praises their daring conduct, and rewards their services with high wages."[16]

While invasion preparations proceeded slowly in the East, the initial U.S, thrust into Canada came from Detroit, near the western end of Lake Erie. In the West enthusiasm for the war was high, state militias were available, and volunteers were plentiful. The British were also vulnerable. The small settlement at Detroit stood west of the Detroit River, across which and to the southeast was Fort Malden, a British outpost lightly defended by a small number of British regulars, volunteers, and Indians. The Americans planned to consolidate their army and militia forces from Ohio and Kentucky at Detroit, cross the river, and seize Fort Malden. From there, they planned to advance against only light resistance along the north shore of Lake Erie to Kingston. Along the way the Americans expected to gain strength through civilian support and Canadian militia deserters.[17]

With an army of U.S. regulars and western militiamen, Major General William Hull marched from Ohio to Detroit. A loyal Jeffersonian Republican, Hull had served effectively as the territorial governor of Michigan. He was also a distinguished Revolutionary War veteran and decades past his military prime. On July 12 his command crossed the Detroit River into British territory opposite Fort Malden. Although Hull's force of 2,200 included only several hundred army regulars, it far outnumbered the fort's defenders. But at age fifty-nine, Hull was a reluctant and tentative commander who hesitated and delayed launching an attack. Fearing for the safety of his supply line into Ohio, the general actually abandoned his offensive and retreated to Detroit on August 8. When General Brock arrived with reinforcements for the threatened garrison, he decided to strike the withdrawing Americans quickly. He crossed into U.S. territory and demanded the surrender of Detroit. Under great stress, Hull had broken down physically and mentally, and without consulting his officers, he surrendered on August 16. To the disgust of many American officers, soldiers, and civilians, the general apparently decided to capitulate because he feared that atrocities might be committed by British Indian allies against the women and children at Detroit. The result was the loss of an entire American army in the West. To make matters worse, both Fort Mackinac, between Lake Huron and Lake Michigan, and Fort Dearborn had fallen. The British now controlled the Detroit River frontier and all of Michigan.[18]

The second prong of the invasion on the Niagara front did not fare any better. In October, after weeks of delay, a mixed American force of around 3,500 army regulars, volunteers, and New York militiamen crossed the Niagara River below Niagara Falls at Queenston. There they scored a temporary victory against a greatly outnumbered enemy force of 2,000 but were defeated when the militia units refused to cross into Canadian territory to assist their compatriots. Among the British dead in the resulting battle was General Brock. In the aftermath of this debacle, the U.S. commander, Brigadier General Alexander Smyth, replaced New York militia major general Stephen Van Rensselaer, but a subsequent assault on Fort Erie in November also failed miserably.

The third and what was originally planned as the major American offensive proved to be a belated and feeble operation. It was not until November that Dearborn gathered a force of more than 6,000 men near Lake Champlain for the march to Montreal. But like their lackluster counterparts, this army also was inexperienced, undisciplined, and poorly led. In spite of the lateness of the season, Dearborn hoped to cross the border and threaten Montreal. Most British troops in the area had already gone into winter quarters when he finally advanced to Champlain near the border in mid-November. His troops then crossed the border and skirmished with the British, but once again the New York militia refused to cross into Canada. Having expected reinforcements from the Niagara operation, Dearborn retreated to New York when he realized that he would not receive any additional support. Despite light casualties, this invasion attempt was a complete fiasco. By November 23, Dearborn was back in Plattsburgh for the winter.[19]

Although the three-prong Canadian offensive had failed miserably, the Madison administration remained confident that American forces would triumph in 1813 after addressing a number of problems that had plagued these operations. John Armstrong had replaced William Eustis as secretary of war. Although he was an abrasive man known for political intrigue, Armstrong was a Revolutionary War veteran who was knowledgeable about military matters and a capable administrator. At the head of the Navy Department, William Jones had replaced Paul Hamilton. A Philadelphia merchant and former congressman, Jones became an energetic and efficient naval secretary who pressed to establish U.S. naval superiority on Lakes Erie, Ontario, and Champlain.

Despite its mishaps in 1812, the United States also continued to enjoy the military advantage in North America. While Britain concentrated on the war against Napoleon, the Americans did not intend to repeat their mistakes. Now the inexperienced regulars who remained in the service had survived their initial combat tests and increasingly proved to be seasoned troops. Younger, more experienced, and tougher officers had also begun to emerge. It would take time for these men to assume command, but positive change was underway.

Confidence was also lifted by the performance of the U.S. Navy and American privateers in 1812. When the war began, most observers had expected the tiny American navy to be quickly swept from the seas by the powerful British fleet. But with the exception of three small vessels, American navy's warships successfully eluded destruction while its heavy frigates scored stunning victories. In August USS *Constitution* (54 guns) had defeated HMS *Guerriere* (49 guns). In October USS *United States* (56 guns) had defeated and captured HMS *Macedonian* (49 guns). In December the *Constitution* had destroyed HMS *Java* (49 guns). Several smaller warships had also scored victories. Meanwhile, to the annoyance of British pride, American privateers effectively preyed on enemy merchant ships. Cruising primarily in Canadian and West Indian waters, these vessels captured hundreds of prizes during 1812.

The administration was slow, however, to solve the problem of senior leadership in the army. Generals Hull, Van Rensselaer, and Smyth had each been sacked or had resigned by the end of 1812. In the West a capable and aggressive officer, Major General William Henry Harrison, had taken charge. In the East, however, the situation did not improve. General Dearborn did not relinquish his command until July 1813. The War Department then named Major General James Wilkinson to take charge of the northern theater and sent Major General Wade Hampton to Lake Champlain to command the army there. But these generals represented more of the same.

Fifty-six-year-old Wilkinson and sixty-two-year-old Hampton were experienced but undistinguished officers well past their primes. In fact, some historians consider Wilkinson to have been one of the worst generals in American history.[20]

In 1813 the Madison administration planned to concentrate offensive operations on Lake Ontario and the Niagara frontier as well as to mount another attack on Montreal. In the West the administration hoped to fight a holding action to protect U.S. soil from British and Indian attacks. But the new commander there was a young, aggressive officer with other plans. After he took command in the fall of 1812, General Harrison immediately began to strengthen, reorganize, and increase the western army with the objective of eventually retaking Detroit from the British and Indian coalition. Between January and August 1813, his rejuvenated forces fought a number of engagements in which they defended American strongholds against enemy attacks.

By 1813, both the Americans and British realized that naval control of Lakes Erie and Ontario was critical to land operations on the Detroit and Niagara frontiers. As a result, both sides began serious ship-building efforts. On Lake Erie the British began the year with a clear advantage, but by August the U.S. commander, twenty-seven-year-old Master Commandant Oliver Hazard Perry, had been able to build a fleet that controlled the lake. When the American ships forced a shortage of food and provisions by disrupting the British supply route, Captain Robert Barclay challenged Perry's squadron on September 10 near Put-in-Bay on western Lake Erie. In the bloody and hard-fought Battle of Lake Erie, the U.S. Navy won a decisive victory. With Fort Malden now completely cut off from its supply line to the east, the British began a hurried retreat that ended with their rout by American forces at the Battle of the Thames in October. In that action the Americans killed the Indian leader Tecumseh and regained control of the Detroit frontier.[21]

Yet control of Lake Ontario and the Niagara frontier remained contested. On Lake Ontario American naval commander Isaac Chauncey and his British counterpart, Commodore Sir James Yeo, engaged in an indecisive shipbuilding contest. Unable to gain control of the lake, both sides conducted periodic raids, with the Americans attacking York (Toronto) on two occasions, while the British struck Sackets Harbor. Along the Niagara frontier, the British temporarily evacuated several strongholds but then retook them by the end of the year.

Meanwhile, a major attack on Montreal again failed to materialize from Lake Champlain. Secretary of War Armstrong planned a two-pronged offensive in which one American force would descend the Saint Lawrence River toward Montreal while the other marched on the city from Lake Champlain. But the operation was poorly planned and mismanaged. The most important problem was senior command. Wilkinson was to lead the U.S. force down the Saint Lawrence while Hampton commanded the advance from Lake Champlain. Both generals were inept, and Wilkinson was apparently partially disabled by his reliance on laudanum (opium). Failure was probably inevitable. With an army of 8,000 men, Wilkinson did not begin his descent of the Saint Lawrence until early November. Less than a week later, a small British force repulsed the Americans in fierce fighting at Crysler's Farm. Hampton's army of 4,000 troops began its march from Plattsburgh in September. By October, it had reached the Chateaugay River, where a small Canadian and British force defeated the Americans on the twenty-fifth. Hampton then returned to Plattsburgh, Wilkinson joining him there after learning of his retreat.[22]

By the end of 1813, the United States had wasted two campaign seasons attempting to invade Canada. A combination of poor preparation, bad planning, largely incompetent civilian and military leadership, and poorly trained troops produced repeated failures. But despite its many missteps and military failures, the United States had not yet been seriously endangered, its homeland largely untouched by the enemy. Raids on American targets had been only sporadic and temporary along the Canadian border and in Chesapeake Bay. Since the British had imposed only a partial blockade, U.S. merchant ships continued to get to sea. Along the New England coast and its border with Canada, illegal trade thrived. And while the Royal Navy dominated the seas, the U.S. Navy had startled the enemy with dramatic victories. Moreover, scores of American privateers had damaged both the enemy's pride and its overseas commerce.

The virtual stalemate ended in 1814 with the changed military situation in Europe. The previous summer at Vittoria, the Duke of Wellington had broken Napoleon's hold on the Iberian Peninsula. Then in October, the emperor's defeat at the Battle of Leipzig forced him to retreat into France. The Allies pursued and entered Paris on March 31. Napoleon abdicated and was sent into exile a short time later. The French defeat meant the British could now concentrate on

North America. Although the war against the United States was an irritating distraction, British leaders and newspapers had been infuriated by the American declaration of war in 1812. They believed that their government had shown considerable restraint in dealing with unreasonable U.S. grievances at a time of great crisis for the kingdom. How, they fumed, could a country of their kinsmen come to the aid of such a monster as Napoleon? With Napoleon "consigned to infamy, there is no public feeling in this country stronger than that of indignation against the Americans," noted *The Times* of London. "That a republic boasting of its freedom should have stooped to become the tool of the Monster's ambition . . . is conduct so black, so loathsome, so hateful, that it naturally stirs up the indignation that we have described." Now it was time to retaliate, peace could wait until the Americans were taught a lesson they would not soon forget. The British were "determined to give Jonathan a good drubbing." Vice Admiral Sir Alexander Cochrane, commander of British naval forces in North America, spoke for many when he stated, "I have it much at heart . . . to give [the Americans] a complete drubbing before peace is made." The London *Sun* insisted on a "peace such as America *deserves*, and British *generosity* may bestow upon . . . a faithless, unprincipled, and corrupt Government." As a result of this "drubbing," Cochrane expected "their northern limits will be circumscribed and the command of the Mississippi wrested from them." "Chastise the savages," demanded *The Times*, "for such they are, in a much truer sense, than the followers of Tecumseh or the Prophet."[23]

Although the government's stance was not as hostile as British public opinion, it confidently conducted an aggressive war in North America. The Earl of Liverpool had been prime minister since May 1812. His Tory administration was ably assisted by Foreign Minister Viscount Robert Castlereagh and Secretary for War and the Colonies Lord Henry Bathurst. While Castlereagh oversaw diplomacy, Bathurst was responsible for managing the war in North America. After Napoleon's defeat, the Liverpool government took several steps to escalate the overseas war. First, the navy would tighten and extend its blockade of the U.S. coast. Second, the government planned to send thousands of reinforcements to Canada, where offensives would be launched to retake the Detroit frontier, secure the Niagara frontier, invade the Lake Champlain region, and occupy parts of Maine. Third, to support their operations in Canada,

British forces would conduct a large diversionary offensive in the Chesapeake Bay area. Later, in the summer of 1814, the British would also activate a plan to campaign in the Gulf of Mexico and capture New Orleans.[24]

In fact, the United States stood unprepared and vulnerable to these offensive operations. After their initial successes, American warships had great difficulty even getting to sea in 1814. Virtually the entire Atlantic coastline thus lay undefended. Along the Canadian border, an increasing number of American army units had fought well, but they had not yet been tested by the thousands of British reinforcements who would arrive from Europe that summer. In Washington the Madison administration continued to provide weak leadership. Finally, the economy floundered, meaning that the government might run out of money during the year to wage the war.

Some had expected that the end of the war in Europe would produce peace with Britain. But more realistic Americans felt that the course of their own conflict had taken a dangerous turn. In London Albert Gallatin observed that the United States now stood alone against a formidable and angry power. British popular support for the war combined with American military weakness and New England's opposition to continued fighting "might prove vitally fatal to the United States." By this he meant not a war of British conquest but possibly the "dissolution of the Union." "Extravagant projects and hopes of success are entertained," Gallatin reported to Secretary of State Monroe. "The restriction of our commerce and fisheries . . . , the curtailment of our northern boundary and an exclusive right to navigate the Lakes . . . , and even a division of the Union is expected from a continuance of the war. The popular feeling is evidently strong in favor of the prosecution of the war against us. This sentiment is universal."[25]

Clearly, the character of the war had changed. "We should have to fight hereafter," wrote Maryland lawyer Joseph Nicholson, "not for 'free Trade and sailors rights,' not for the Conquest of the Canadas, but for our own national existence." The slogan "Don't give up the ship" was now replaced by a more ominous one, "Don't give up the soil." The United States was no longer fighting to invade Canada but rather to protect itself from invasion. If they succeeded, the British clearly intended to demand American territory as the price of peace.[26] A genuine national crisis loomed.

CHAPTER 2

THE CHAMPLAIN VALLEY IN THE WAR OF 1812

When the War of 1812 had begun, Lake Champlain seemed certain to play a critical role in the conflict. This had been the case in both the French-Indian War and the American Revolution because it stood at the heart of the Great Warpath, the military corridor that stretched roughly 200 miles from Ticonderoga, New York, to Montreal. Also making Lake Champlain strategically important was its length (120 miles) and adjacent topography. Densely forested hills and mountains rose from both shores of the lake, where the few existing roads were narrow and rough. Although small wagons and carts carried goods and materials on these roads, the commerce of the region moved primarily by water. By 1800, lake traffic between points such as Burlington, Vermont, and Plattsburgh, New York, was brisk. Beginning in 1809, Champlain supported the second steamship in the United States. The fact that transportation and commerce relied heavily on it in peacetime meant that naval control of the lake would be critical to supporting large numbers of troops in wartime.

But Lake Champlain remained a military backwater for more than two years after hostilities commenced because virtually all of the major fighting along the border between Canada and the United States occurred elsewhere. In 1812 the expected American attack on Montreal from Lake Champlain had not materialized until the end of the campaign season, which then proved to be brief, feeble, and anticlimactic. In 1813 Champlain again played a secondary role to events on Lakes Erie and Ontario. Although there was sporadic naval activity, neither the Americans nor the British established a major force on the lake. And as in 1812, the U.S. military buildup occurred slowly and produced only a half-hearted and unsuccessful invasion in the fall. Lake Champlain finally became a critical military theater only in 1814 once the British decided to wrest control from the Americans by mounting a major invasion of the region.

Despite its strategic importance, the population and economy of the Champlain Valley had grown slowly in the decades after the American Revolution. The region was sparsely populated, economically undeveloped, and not directly connected by a navigable waterway to either the Saint Lawrence River to the north or the Hudson River to the south. In 1810 roughly 3,000 people lived in Burlington on the eastern shore. An estimated 61,000 people lived in the New York shore counties. One of these, Clinton County, which became the main theater of operations, had a population of only 8,000. The border town of Champlain, New York, had only 1,200 residents, while Plattsburgh, the strategic gateway to the valley, had 3,112 residents. The latter village had seventy-eight houses, a courthouse, two newspapers, and more than two dozen stores, shops, and offices as well as a tannery and several mills. A large number of military supplies were also stored there.[1]

In the two decades before 1812, the economy of the Champlain Valley achieved a "modest prosperity" that connected American and Canadian border communities and linked both to the markets of Montreal and Quebec. The Richelieu River furnished the key link because only a ten-mile section of the river between Saint-Jean and Chambly was not navigable to small vessels. Trade grew steadily as Americans shipped potash, farm goods, and timber products to Canada while importing British manufactured goods and various items such as furs. This commerce produced a strong cross-border economic community that transcended tariffs, trade restrictions, and even war. By 1807, the value of trade at the Saint-Jean custom house totaled more than 200,000 British pounds. When President Jefferson's embargo went into effect the following year, legitimate trade dropped dramatically but illegal smuggling boomed.[2] Many Americans and Canadians near the border resented and ignored the embargo because it threatened to destroy their economic lifeline. In 1809 an estimated $400,000 worth of goods were smuggled out of the Champlain Valley into Canada, and an estimated $200,000 worth of goods entered the valley illegally from the north. In the remaining years before the War of 1812, these figures continued to increase.[3]

When war began in June 1812, public response was mixed at best, with Americans in the northern Champlain Valley reacting with uncertainty and fear. They immediately pleaded with local and state officials for protection. In response, the local militias were called out until it became clear that there was no threat of an attack from Canada. Soon residents tried to go about their lives as if the war did not exist. Widespread smuggling resumed as local foodstuffs, natural resources, and livestock readily found their way across the northern border.

In the summer of 1812, the region did not become a major theater for military operations. Governor in Chief Prevost's defensive plans to protect Lower Canada meant that he had no intention of attacking the Champlain Valley. Meanwhile, the Madison administration was in no position to mount an immediate offensive from Lake Champlain. There was virtually no U.S. naval presence. With the navy's two gunboats there in disrepair, the local naval commander, Lieutenant Sidney Smith, had no force to command until he managed to repair and arm one of the vessels. In addition, it took several months for the Americans to raise troops for an invasion. Beyond the local militias, there were few available regular soldiers. Moreover, even if the troops had been at hand, the very rural, sparsely settled, and relatively isolated valley was completely unprepared for a major military buildup. There were virtually no fortifications or military facilities at either Plattsburgh or Burlington. Since even crude barracks were not completed until December, when troops finally began to assemble, they spent a depressing fall sleeping in tents exposed to cold and rainy weather.[4]

Moreover, the senior commander of the northern theater, Major General Dearborn, moved slowly. Early in the war, Dearborn had established his headquarters in Greenbush, New York, then traveled to New York City to oversee defenses there, and then visited New England on an unsuccessful mission to recruit troops for the invasion. When he learned that the British had repealed their Orders-in-Council, Dearborn and Prevost agreed to an armistice in early August in the hope that the war would end before serious fighting erupted in their region. President Madison rejected the truce, which ended officially on September 3, but valuable weeks had been lost. When Dearborn finally arrived in Burlington in October, he found American military preparations in disarray. In command was fifty-nine-year-old Brigadier General Joseph Bloomfield, who had served in the American Revolution. A longtime politician, he was the current governor of New Jersey. As a Federalist, Bloomfield had been appointed to bolster political support for the war, but he quickly proved to be inept as a general. One observer in Burlington noted that the governor was "better qualified to surrender an army into the hands of the enemy than to conduct one triumphantly to victory and conquest." When Bloomfield resigned in October because of poor health, American forces were still weeks away from being ready for an invasion.[5]

American naval weakness on Lake Champlain began to change in October, when Lieutenant Thomas Macdonough arrived to take command. Although he was only twenty-eight years old, Macdonough already had achieved a distinguished service record. On the *Constellation* during the Quasi-War, he had participated in the capture of the French frigate *L'Insurgente* in 1798. Then during the Barbary Wars, Macdonough had served on the *Philadelphia*, though he was not on board when the frigate was captured by Tripoli. But he was part of the small unit under Lieutenant Stephen Decatur that subsequently boarded and burned the *Philadelphia*, an exploit generally recognized as one of the most heroic actions of that era. In the Mediterranean he had been one of "Preble's Boys," demonstrating courage in combat and mastering important naval skills.[6]

Macdonough was exceptionally well qualified for his new duties. He was recognized as a resourceful and energetic officer who believed in careful preparation and detailed planning. Personally, Macdonough was a devout Episcopalian known for his impeccable moral conduct. Himself a religious man, Eleazer Williams commented that the lieutenant was the only navy officer he had found to be "pious, and attends upon the divine institutions." Never a colorful or flamboyant officer, Macdonough was nevertheless a leader whom his men worshipped and willingly followed. His personal character, professional abilities, and admirable conduct combined to mark an outstanding leader.[7]

Since he had supervised the construction of gunboats during his career, Macdonough also brought shipbuilding and logistical knowledge. This expertise was immediately called upon when he reached Burlington on October 8, learning upon his arrival that the skeletal condition of the American squadron left a great deal to be done. The two gunboats were now operational and six sloops had been purchased, but they were an uneven lot. The *President*, the *Hunter* (renamed the *Growler*), and the *Bull Dog* (renamed the *Eagle*) had been converted into naval vessels, but they still needed to be equipped, armed, and manned. The other three sloops ended up acting as army transport vessels because their old hulls were not strong enough to be armed. Macdonough also built more than one hundred bateaux. These unarmed thirty-five- to forty-foot rowboats were designed to transport men and supplies across the lake. Since the British had only several small gunboats at Isle-aux-Noix in the Richelieu River, the Americans controlled the lake. Macdonough's warships patrolled the northern end of the lake and protected the transports. Unthreatened by the enemy, American vessels carried men and supplies across the lake as preparation for the fall invasion of Canada.

When the American operation finally occurred in November, it was a dismal failure. Most of the 6,000–8,000 men who assembled at Burlington and Plattsburgh were inexperienced, poorly trained, and inadequately equipped. Not surprisingly, the health and morale of the troops were poor. Given the circumstances, Dearborn would have preferred not to invade, but he had been under pressure from Washington since July to act. "Go to Albany or the Lake [Champlain]! The troops shall come to you as fast as the season will admit, and the blow must be struck," wrote Secretary of War Eustis. "Congress must not meet without a victory to announce to them." Hull's disastrous surrender of Detroit in August and the American failure at Queenston in October had intensified the pressure for a successful offensive.[8]

As a result, the reluctant Dearborn felt compelled to advance with his ill-prepared army. One militia officer in Plattsburgh wrote that his unit was about to "march without baggage or tents, and everything we carry will be on our backs, and the Heavens and a blanket our only covering." One of the few bright spots for Dearborn was the assistance of Colonel Zebulon Pike, who led a detachment of four hundred regulars from western New York. An able field officer, Pike had distinguished himself by leading two army exploration missions to the far west between 1805 and 1807.[9]

On November 16 the invasion force began its march north. Dearborn joined the army and took direct command at Champlain, where he was informed that some of the militia units refused to cross the border. Nevertheless, the next day a detachment led by Pike forded the Lacolle River and attacked an outpost manned by a small force of Canadians and Indians. The defenders fled as the Americans set the guardhouse on fire. In the meantime, another detachment had forded the river and approached the guardhouse from a different direction. When these Americans came upon Pike's men, they mistook them for the enemy and opened fire. After thirty confused minutes, both American groups retreated back across the river, leaving behind two dead, thirteen wounded, and five missing. After this disastrous start, Dearborn decided to abandon his offensive. In his mind the risks of continuing outweighed the potential rewards. The American army was back in nearby Champlain on November 22, and the next day it marched for Plattsburgh and Burlington, where the troops went into winter quarters.

This ended the 1812 campaign season. In Plattsburgh and Burlington, the troops suffered through a long and miserable winter, during which many died from illness; the death rate was an estimated 10 percent for the troops stationed in Plattsburgh and 12.5 percent for those in Burlington. Meanwhile, Macdonough withdrew his vessels south to Shelburne Bay, where he spent most of the winter refitting and adding to his small squadron. His personal respite came in December, when the young officer took a temporary leave to get married in Middletown, Connecticut.[10]

As he worked to strengthen his squadron, Macdonough had a major advantage: British access to Lake Champlain was limited to a narrow neck at its northern end where it emptied into the Richelieu River. While the British were bottled up at their small base at Isle-aux-Noix, Macdonough could draw on Burlington, Vergennes, Plattsburgh, and other U.S. settlements for resources and supplies. He also acquired and converted several ships owned by civilians. Over the winter, Macdonough recruited workers, arranged for the purchase and shipment of the provisions needed to outfit his vessels, obtained guns with which to arm them, and attempted to find recruits to fill his crews. Always energetic and resourceful, he solved most of his material challenges. Ample lumber was available to build new ships and refit existing ones. Small forges and foundries were available in Burlington and Vergennes for metalwork. Naval provisions, guns, and ordnance were shipped from New York and New England.[11]

Macdonough's major problem was not outfitting his ships, but crewing them. Manpower remained a serious and persistent problem throughout the war. In addition to the lack of popular support for the conflict in the immediate area, naval duty on small ships on a freshwater lake did not appeal to most men willing to serve. Instead, they much preferred duty with their local militia unit or to volunteer for the army, where they received larger recruitment bonuses than Macdonough could offer. For those attracted to the navy, though, duty on large, oceangoing warships seemed much more attractive than that on smaller vessels on a relatively small lake, where many sailors suffered from various illnesses. Service at sea was not only more glamorous, it also offered the prospect of prize money. On Lake Champlain this bonus seemed out of the question. As a result, it was only in a halting and fitful way that Macdonough manned his squadron over the next two years. On several occasions he removed vessels from frontline duty so that he could transfer some of their men to units about to go into action.

As it had in 1812, Lake Champlain remained a military backwater for most of 1813. In March Dearborn's army was transferred from Plattsburgh and Burlington to Lake Ontario because the Madison administration had decided to concentrate its land forces on the Niagara frontier and Lake Ontario. Although this decision left northern Lake Champlain as defenseless as it had been at the beginning of the war, the situation did not seem dangerous because Macdonough controlled the water. His squadron now consisted of the *Growler* and the *Eagle*, with eleven guns each; the *President*, with twelve guns; and two gunboats, with one gun each. Bottled up at the northern end of the lake, the several British gunboats could not come close to matching Macdonough's thirty-six-gun force.

But the naval situation changed dramatically during the spring of 1813. In April the *President* was seriously damaged when it ran aground near Plattsburgh. The following month one of the gunboats capsized in Cumberland Bay. Then in early June, disaster struck. Under the command of Lieutenant Sidney Smith, the *Growler* and the *Eagle* aggressively pursued British gunboats to the north end of the lake. Against Macdonough's orders, Smith crossed the border and entered the narrow neck leading to the head of the Richelieu River and Isle-aux-Noix. The Americans had a superior force but realized too late that they were trapped. Against a light wind from the south and pushed by a current running north, Smith had little room to maneuver when his vessels were fired on from shore and from gunboats. A spirited fight ensued, but when it was over, the *Eagle* had been sunk in shallow water and the *Growler* forced to surrender. Although casualties were light, the British captured almost one hundred Americans, marching them first to Montreal and then to Quebec as prisoners. Among those captured was Lieutenant Smith, who would be exonerated by a board of inquiry two years later. The British quickly repaired and renamed the two captured ships.

The HMS *Blake* and HMS *Shannon* thereafter controlled the northern end of the lake.[12]

Angered by what he considered to be the impetuous behavior of Smith, Macdonough had little choice but to retreat south to Burlington to regroup. His objective now was to regain naval control of the lake. "You are to understand that on no account are you to suffer the enemy to gain the ascendancy on Lake Champlain," wrote Secretary of the Navy Jones, "and you have unlimited authority to procure the necessary resources for men, materials and munitions for that purpose."[13] As a result, Macdonough received permission to purchase and equip two additional sloops and build four gunboats. At the end of July, the Navy Department also promoted Macdonough to commander (or master commandant). Since he was in charge of a multiship squadron, Macdonough now also carried the title of commodore, which in the early U.S. Navy was a purely honorary title rather than an official rank. Macdonough acted quickly, but it was not until September that he had finished rebuilding his squadron. It now consisted of the *President*, the *Preble*, the *Montgomery*, and four gunboats. He had also acquired two other sloops, the *Frances* and the *Wasp*, but they proved unworthy, poor-sailing vessels that he later relinquished.[14]

Meanwhile, a new troop buildup had begun at Burlington in July 1813. After U.S. offensives on the Niagara frontier and on Lake Ontario had failed, the Madison administration decided to launch a two-pronged joint offensive against Montreal. One army, under Major General Wilkinson, would move from Sackets Harbor to the head of the Saint Lawrence River and then descend to Montreal. Meanwhile, the other wing of the attack, commanded by Major General Hampton, would march north from Lake Champlain. Unfortunately, from the outset the invasion had little chance of success due to poor planning and inept leadership. Wilkinson and Hampton were not only weak commanders but also despised each other. Hampton bluntly refused to serve under, cooperate with, or take orders from Wilkinson, instead, only taking orders directly from Secretary of War Armstrong. Clearly, the likelihood of a well-planned or executed campaign was remote under these circumstances.

When Hampton arrived in July, there were about 4,000 troops at Burlington. In addition to his contempt for militia units, the general quickly became very unpopular with his own soldiers, many of whom he disdained as untrained and undisciplined. From his headquarters in Burlington, he also rejected appeals to send troops across the lake to Plattsburgh and the border town of Champlain, where local leaders realized that they were defenseless. Since there were no regulars stationed in these towns and the British navy now controlled the lake, these villages could be raided at will by the enemy.[15]

Meanwhile in Canada, Governor in Chief Prevost became increasingly concerned about Lake Champlain as he received reports about the U.S. military buildup in Burlington. While temporarily enjoying naval control, he decided in July to raid Lake Champlain. His goal was to gain military intelligence, destroy public buildings and stores, create general havoc, and divert pressure from Upper Canada. Prevost sent Lieutenant Colonel John Murray with more than nine hundred officers and men to Isle-aux-Noix. British naval forces for the operation were commanded by Captain Thomas Everard from the HMS *Wasp*, with Captain Daniel Pring second in command. Everard had volunteered for temporary duty to lead eighty of his men on the operation.[16]

On July 29 the expedition headed south from Isle-aux-Noix. It consisted of the sloops *Broke* and *Shannon*, three gunboats, and forty-seven bateaux to transport Murray's force. Meanwhile in Plattsburgh, New York militia general Mooers had appealed futilely to General Hampton for troops from Burlington. When Hampton refused, local leaders met with Mooers on the morning of July 31 to request that he "not put up resistance, which could destroy the town." Later that day the British landed unopposed, Mooers having hurriedly evacuated his three hundred militiamen from the village.[17]

Murray's troops entered Plattsburgh unopposed and burned the arsenal, a blockhouse, warehouses, and barracks as well as plundered and looted private property and homes. After capturing a small private sloop and burning a blockhouse on Cumberland Head, the British departed on August 1, splitting into two groups. One force, under Colonel Murray, sailed north, landing first at Point au Roche and then at Swanton, Vermont, where it destroyed more public and private property. Under Everard and Pring, the second British force, which consisted of the *Broke* and *Shannon* and a galley, headed for Burlington, which they briefly bombarded from long range on August 2. After American shore guns and vessels anchored close in returned fire, the squadron sailed for Shelburne Bay and Charlotte, Vermont, before returning to base. In the process Captain Everard reported that his ships had captured or destroyed four vessels, including the privately owned fifty-ton *Essex*. On the return to Canada, one British detachment plundered stores at Chazy while another marched to Champlain, New York, and burned two block-houses, a storehouse, and a barracks. This brief but effective raid dramatically demonstrated the need for U.S. naval control of Lake Champlain and for the presence of American troops in Plattsburgh.

Despite his mishaps earlier in 1813, Macdonough had quickly rebuilt his squadron and reentered Lake Champlain in early September with five armed sloops and two gunboats. Two more gunboats were added in October. Although the margin was slight, Macdonough had regained the edge. When the American warships sailed to the north end of the lake, the British vessels retreated over the border into the Richelieu River. With one brief exception in December, Macdonough's patrols prevented any further enemy raids. His job now was to support the troop buildup for another planned invasion of Canada.[18]

According to Secretary of War Armstrong's plan, Hampton would march north from Lake Champlain to Montreal while Wilkinson's army would approach the city by descending the Saint Lawrence River from Lake Ontario. Hampton initially intended to move his army down the Richelieu, but Macdonough vetoed the idea because of the British military and naval strength at Isle-Aux-Noix. Instead, the general decided to bypass the enemy stronghold and head west from Champlain. Macdonough's main job was to prevent the British squadron from reentering Lake Champlain and disrupting the movement of American troops along the lake. Otherwise, Macdonough's vessels convoyed those boats carrying American troops from Cumberland Head to the mouth of the Great Chazy River near Champlain. By September 20, Hampton's poorly trained and inexperienced army of more than 4,000 troops had reached the town. After an abortive first attempt to cross the border, Hampton decided to follow the Chateaugay River, which empties into the Saint Lawrence not far from Montreal. But instead of advancing on his own, he waited and waited for news of Wilkinson's progress. After nearly a month without word from the general, Hampton finally ordered a short-lived advance on October 21. Five days later the Americans met a much smaller force of about 1,700 Canadians supported by a few Indians. In the ensuing Battle of Chateaugay, the Canadians thoroughly con-fused and defeated the Americans, who retreated across the border to Chateaugay, a town in New York, and then back to Plattsburgh.[19]

Meanwhile, after beginning its descent of the Saint Lawrence in early November, Wilkinson's 8,000-man army met a similar fate. A British force of 800 troops engaged and decisively defeated an American detachment in the Battle of Crysler's Farm. In response, Wilkinson fell back on November 12 and then went into winter quarters. Blaming Hampton for the failure, Wilkinson tried to have him arrested for disobedience, but the general fled New York and returned to Washington. The 1813 invasion of Canada was over. In a final footnote to the year's activities, Captain Pring led a surprise naval raid on December 4. The British landed and burned an empty storehouse on Cumberland Head before four U.S. vessels unsuccessfully pursued them back across the border. Shortly thereafter, on December 21, Macdonough brought his ships to Vergennes, Vermont, for the winter.

Although his 1813 campaign had been a fiasco, Wilkinson remained unbowed. He determined to restore his reputation and his army's good name with a late-winter or early spring operation against Montreal. Despite contravening advice from his officers, the general decided to bypass Isle-aux-Noix and march his 4,000-man army down the west side of the Richelieu River toward the city. His first objective was Lacolle Mill on the Lacolle River five miles southwest of Isle-aux-Noix. The mill was actually a three-story fortification with thick walls defended by 200 regulars, who during the ensuing engagement were supported by several hundred reinforcements. On March 30 the Americans attacked, but because soft ground prevented bringing heavy guns to bear, they failed to damage the fort and retired at the end of the day after suffering more than 250 casualties. This latest debacle brought an end to Wilkinson's tenure.

Meanwhile, during the winter, a serious contest for the naval control of Lake Champlain developed. Although neither the Americans nor the British had definite plans for the 1814 campaign season, both sides now understood that naval control of the lake was critical. Macdonough's objective was to build a force that would prevent raids on American settlements on the shoreline by keeping the British bottled up in the Richelieu River. To this end, Vergennes furnished an excellent winter base for Macdonough and his preparations. Located south of Burlington and seven miles up Otter Creek, the town was less vulnerable than Shelburne Bay. The Otter could be fortified at its mouth and handle ships displacing up to 750 tons. With a peacetime population of eight hundred, Vergennes had eight forges, a blast furnace, an air furnace, various mills, a nail shop, and a wire factory. It also contained a shipyard and the Monkton Iron Works, which agreed to furnish iron fittings as well as land for Macdonough to build a shipyard. Stands of oak and pine as well as beds of iron ore were also readily available. Vergennes was connected by road to Boston and Burlington as well as by stage roads to Rutland and Whitehall, which connected with routes to Albany and Boston.[20]

In December Secretary of the Navy Jones had instructed Macdonough to build fifteen seventy-five-foot gunboats (also known as row galleys). These vessels were considered to be the most effective way to combat the increasing number of gunboats in the British squadron. In fact, gunboats were ideal for service on Lake Champlain. These shallow-draft vessels were easy and cheap to build. Driven by oars, they were fast, did not depend on the wind, and could operate in shallow water. But their utility was limited by the large number of men required to row them, and they were easily outclassed by larger, more heavily armed warships.[21]

The British had also determined to gain naval control of the lake. Prevost wanted a force that would not only protect his base at Isle-aux-Noix but also sustain his ability to conduct naval raids along the shoreline. After they had captured the two American sloops and successfully raided Plattsburgh and other targets, the British decided to convert Isle-aux-Noix into a naval as well as a military base. In response, Captain Pring created a shipyard and asked permission to build two gunboats as well as a new brig. Prevost approved construction of the two gunboats but temporarily delayed work on the brig, meaning the new 16-gun HMS *Linnet* was not ready until May 1814. Prevost also dispatched William Simmons from Kingston to Isle-aux-Noix to supervise construction there. To strengthen its defenses, additional outposts were added as well as a barracks, hospital, and storehouses. The British also built a large dry dock protected by gates that opened and closed. When Commodore Yeo visited the base in February 1814, he found it to be in good order.[22]

In January 1814 Macdonough learned from spies that the British were building a large warship at Isle-aux-Noix. To counter this threat, Secretary Jones gave him the option of building either the fifteen gunboats or of constructing one large warship along with three or four gunboats. Since the objective was to "have no doubt of your commanding the lake," Macdonough decided to build a large sloop and was "therefore authorized to employ such means and workmen as shall render its accomplishment certain."[23]

To build Macdonough's squadron, the Navy Department contracted with Adam and Noah Brown of New York City. The Browns were known as outstanding shipwrights for their record of building fast, seaworthy vessels quickly. Already the Browns had built a number of fast, high-quality privateers during the war. In 1813 the navy had hired Noah Brown to build Oliver Hazard Perry's squadron on Lake Erie. Under harsh and difficult conditions, Brown built two 20-gun brigs, three gunboats, and a dispatch schooner. Several months later the two brigs, the *Lawrence* and the *Niagara*, were vital in decisively defeating the British in the Battle of Lake Erie. After returning to New York, the Browns built the highly regarded 20-gun sloop *Peacock* for the U.S. Navy.

In February 1814 the Browns scrambled to collect the men and equipment necessary to build a 26-gun warship and six gunboats for Macdonough. At Vergennes, with a large workforce and ample supplies of timber and iron, construction proceeded quickly. Just forty days after work began, the 26-gun sloop of war *Saratoga* was launched into Otter Creek on April 11. It took another three weeks to finish the rigging, mount the guns, and supply provisions. The six gunboats were also launched by the end of April.

Secretary Jones also authorized Macdonough to acquire and outfit an unfinished steamship at Vergennes. If completed as a steamship, the vessel would have been the first steam-powered warship in the world. But Macdonough had serious doubts about utilizing steam to drive a warship. Since all of the necessary machinery was not available, a construction delay of two months would result. Reliability was also a problem. Macdonough noted that the only steamship then operating on the lake rarely crossed without a mechanical problem putting it out of service until parts could be ordered and delivered from Albany. Moreover, its estimated five-knot speed would be exceeded by the six-knot speed of the enemy's galleys. As a result, Macdonough and Brown decided to convert the hull into a sail-powered schooner. Brown and his men began work in late April and launched the *Ticonderoga* on May 12. To furnish the schooner's seventeen guns, Macdonough stripped four of his old gunboats and removed guns from his two inferior sloops, the *Frances* and the *Wasp*.[24]

While construction on his new ships proceeded quickly, Macdonough continued to be plagued by his inability to recruit. He suggested to Secretary Jones during construction that men should be transferred from the navy's oceangoing warships. "I much fear when I get my vessels in other respects, ready for service, there will be a great want of men." As a result of this and other issues, Macdonough reorganized and reduced his squadron. Since the sloops *Frances* and *Wasp* were poor sailors, he returned them to their civilian owners. He also removed most of the guns from the *President* and *Montgomery* and converted them into transport vessels. As a result, Macdonough's squadron now consisted of the flagship *Saratoga*, the *Ticonderoga*, the 7-gun *Preble*, and the new gunboats.[25] Nevertheless, he still lacked enough men for his ships. Despite Macdonough's appeals, Secretary Jones refused to transfer men from other stations or to take other steps to furnish additional sailors. Meanwhile, as the naval commander waited for men to arrive from his recruiting stations, the army refused to loan him soldiers. By early May, the ice was gone from the lake, but Macdonough's ships still waited at Vergennes.

Meanwhile, military events in Europe had changed the character of the war in North America and, by so doing, underscored the importance and urgency of the naval race on Lake Champlain. With the defeat and abdication of Napoleon in early April 1814, the Liverpool government decided to send thousands of veteran troops to Canada to invade U.S. territory. Two weeks after Napoleon's defeat, the secretary for war and the colonies, Lord Bathurst, informed Prevost that the government was taking advantage of the favorable situation in Europe to send "military and artillery" reinforcements to Quebec "as soon as they can be collected." A high-ranking military official, Colonel Henry Torrens, reported that the Liverpool government had ordered "Lord Wellington to prepare a corps of 12,000 infantry and a small detachment of cavalry to be sent to America." When dispatched, these reinforcements included four companies of artillery, one regiment of cavalry, and fourteen battalions of infantry. Once in Canada, these units were to attack American bases on Lakes Erie, Ontario, and Champlain.[26]

In anticipation of victory in Europe, the Liverpool government had already asked the duke to recommend the best strategy for the American war. Wellington responded that since the defense of Canada depended upon control of the "navigation of the lakes. . . . Any offensive operations founded upon Canada must be preceded by the establishment of naval superiority on the lakes." Given its size, sparse population, and inability to sustain a large army,

he emphasized that "military operations by large bodies are impracticable, unless the party carrying them on has the uninterrupted use
of a navigable river, or very extensive means of land transport, which
such a country [Canada] can rarely have." Wellington also cautioned
that it would be difficult for Britain to bring enough force to bear
in one "operation which would be so injurious to the Americans
as to force them to suc for peace, which is what one would wish to
see." As a result of the duke's authoritative opinion, naval control
of Lake Champlain now emerged as a pressing and critical British
operational priority.[27]

In April London took more direct control of military operations
in North America. The Liverpool government sent Vice Admiral
Cochrane to replace Admiral John Warren in command of the North
American station. Known to be a more aggressive commander than
Warren, Cochrane was to extend and tighten the naval blockade of
the United States. He was also to create a diversion to assist British
forces in Canada by attacking suitable targets on the U.S. coast,
including those in Chesapeake Bay. To support Cochrane, the government dispatched additional ships and a brigade of troops under
the command of Major General Robert Ross. In instructions dated
June 3, 1814, Lord Bathurst targeted the northern border by ordering Prevost "to commence offensive operations on the Enemy's
Frontier" with the large number of reinforcements being sent from
Europe. These orders specifically identified American naval bases
on Lakes Erie, Ontario, and Champlain as targets to be destroyed.[28]
Meanwhile, from Halifax, Lieutenant General Sir John Sherbrooke
was to attack and occupy enough of the Maine coast to "ensure an
uninterrupted communication between Halifax & Quebec." An
additional strike against U.S. targets in the Gulf of Mexico was also
being contemplated but was not approved until later in 1814.[29]

On Lake Champlain Macdonough did not learn of these developments for several months, though in the meantime, he understood
that his contest for naval control there should continue unabated.
Since Macdonough was not able to bring his squadron onto the lake
until late May, there was concern that Burlington and Vergennes
might be vulnerable to attack. As a result, 1,500 regulars and militiamen were called out to protect the two towns. With their flotilla
located seven miles up Otter Creek, the Americans built Fort Cassin
near the mouth of the creek, manned by army regulars and fortified
by seven navy 12-pounders.

Fears of an enemy attack were realized in early May, when the British won the race to enter the lake first. At Isle-aux-Noix Captain Pring had spent the winter strengthening his squadron, which now included the new 16-gun brig HMS *Linnet*, six sloops, and ten galleys. On May 9 Pring headed up Lake Champlain in the *Linnet*, accompanied by seven gunboats, two merchant sloops, and the two captured American sloops, now renamed the *Broke* and the *Shannon*. The objective of the operation was "attacking the enemy's [naval] force laying in . . . Otter Creek near Vergennes, if found practicable[,] or otherwise to block up the Channel near the entrance."[30] The warships also carried a detachment of marines, which Pring planned to land and either destroy the U.S. ships or block the entrance to Otter Creek by sinking the two merchant sloops there. The British reached Vergennes on May 14 and attacked early the next morning. But the Americans had been warned and were ready when the enemy began shelling Fort Cassin. Since Pring did not have enough marines to take the fort, he withdrew after two hours. The squadron then proceeded to the Bouquet River and captured U.S. government flour stored at a gristmill in Willsboro. Although Pring's raid failed to damage or bottle up the American fleet, he captured two men in a small boat who furnished him with valuable intelligence on the U.S. fleet, including the presence of the *Saratoga* and the *Ticonderoga*. In response, the British escalated their own construction program once they returned to Isle-aux-Noix.

Finally on May 26, Macdonough's fleet left Otter Creek and entered Lake Champlain. It now consisted of six new gunboats and five warships: the *Saratoga*, *Ticonderoga*, *Preble*, *President*, and *Montgomery*. This force did not include four fifty-foot gunboats that had been temporarily disarmed because they lacked sufficient crews and guns. Although still undersized, the American army temporarily loaned the men that the warship crews needed until they could be replaced by new naval recruits. From Plattsburgh, Macdonough sent several vessels to Point au Fer to prevent the British from reentering the lake. Three days later the officer reported that he had been informed that all of the enemy's vessels had returned to Isle-aux-Noix. "There is now a free communication between all parts of this lake," wrote a confident Macdonough, "and at present there is no doubt of this communication being interrupted by the enemy."[31]

For the moment, the Americans controlled the lake, but within a week a new development shook Macdonough's confidence. On June 7 the U.S. commander learned from spies that the British had begun new naval construction at Isle-aux-Noix. In addition, they had reportedly shipped the frames and the parts for four frigates to Montreal, two of which were rumored to be on their way to the Richelieu. Four days later Macdonough learned from British desert-ers that the new vessel under construction was to be a large frigate, exceeding thirty guns, which would be considerably more powerful than the American flagship, the *Saratoga*.

Macdonough immediately responded by requesting authority from the Navy Department to build an additional 18-gun sloop. When he received the request, Secretary Jones refused to autho-rize another warship. Only a month earlier Jones had reported to President Madison that he did not "anticipate anything to dis-turb our complete control on Lake Champlain," convinced that Macdonough already had a sufficient force to prevent the British from entering the lake. "Our superiority will not be placed beyond doubt. Indeed there is good reason to believe the enemy will not ven-ture on the lake."[32] In addition to not trusting Macdonough's assess-ment, Jones sought to avoid another expensive shipbuilding "war of the broad axes" similar to the one underway on Lake Ontario. But in an uncharacteristic act, Madison overruled his secretary and gave his approval for the new warship. Jones complied but remained unconvinced. Several weeks later he complained to the president: "God knows where the money is to come from!" Jones even doubted that the British were building a new vessel and reported that the reports of a frigates-in-frame being sent had been false.[33]

Although the British had begun to build their new frigate two months into spring, construction lagged because they lacked skilled workers, naval supplies, and raw materials at Isle-aux-Noix. One issue for Prevost was the low priority given to the need for naval supplies there by Commodore Yeo, who consistently ordered these scarce resources to be sent to Lake Ontario to support his own naval race with Commodore Chauncey. For example, when London sent the frames, guns, and equipment to build four frigates to Montreal, it was not feasible then to transport the frigates-in-frame to either Lake Ontario or to Lake Champlain. But Yeo ordered that all of the fit-tings and equipment be sent to Lake Ontario to meet his needs there. Although Prevost did not object at the time, he would later complain to London about the lack of support he received at Isle-aux-Noix from the commodore.[34]

As a result of their lack of construction materials from overseas, the British relied on American smugglers to supply some of their needs. To his considerable frustration, Macdonough battled all summer against those Americans who furnished provisions and hundreds of cattle as well as lumber, spars, and other building supplies for the construction of the new British frigate, the *Confiance*. Although they were aware of the problem, U.S. forces had only mixed success in cutting off this enemy source of supply. On June 29 a naval patrol seized two eighty-foot spars that Macdonough understood to be for the fore and mizzen masts of the British warship under construction. Then eight days later, Lieutenant Joel Abbot led a daring mission across the border. Evading sentries, he located several spars being stored on the shore of the Richelieu River. Abbot's men towed the timbers into the river and cut them into pieces.[35] On July 23 the Americans intercepted a "large raft of planks, timber and tar" headed for Canada. With its 13,000 feet of plank and numerous oak timbers and barrels of tar, in Macdonough's mind the material was "unquestionably bound to the enemy." Although these efforts did not stop completely the illegal flow of supplies to Isle-aux-Noix, they did hamper and delay the construction of the *Confiance* and ultimately contributed to the British defeat on Lake Champlain. In addition to such material aid, Macdonough was also exasperated by the information and intelligence that Americans in the area were providing his opponents. "The turpitude of many of our citizens in this part of the country furnishes the enemy with every information he wants," he complained to Washington officials on June 8.[36]

Since the Navy Department sent instructions directly to the New York shipbuilders, Macdonough did not learn of Madison's authorization to build a new warship until Adam Brown arrived at Lake Champlain on July 18. By the time that he met with Macdonough, Brown had already signed up two hundred skilled workers for the project. After discussing the dimensions, armament, and rigging of the vessel, they agreed that it should be built at the Vergennes shipyard. The keel was laid from three timbers on July 23, and construction proceeded quickly. Brown understood that the speed of construction was more important than the long-term durability of the vessel. As a result, he used whatever type of wood was readily available, including white oak, spruce, white pine, elm, chestnut, and oak. Although Macdonough intended to arm the new ship entirely with long 18-pound guns, he eventually had to settle for twelve 32-pound carronades and eight 18-pound long guns.[37] In an amazing feat, the new warship, which would be named the USS *Eagle*, was launched on August 11, just nineteen days after its keel had been laid. Nevertheless, its masts and riggings had yet to be installed, much carpentry work remained to be done, and most of its equipment, including sails, guns, gun carriages, shot, powder, and other essentials, had not yet arrived. But the Americans were now close to winning the latest round in their naval race because HMS *Confiance* was still weeks away from launching.

As with the other American ships, manpower was a problem for the *Eagle*. The Navy Department dispatched Master Commandant Robert Henley to be the new commander. His first lieutenant was Joseph Smith, who had been the second lieutenant on the *Saratoga*. Rather than complain and make manpower requests that could not be filled, the resourceful Smith went to work himself to fill his ship's crew. First, Macdonough agreed to transfer forty men from the *Saratoga*. Smith was permitted to select twenty men while the other twenty were to be chosen by the *Saratoga*'s first lieutenant. As a result, the *Eagle* ended up with twenty "good men" as well as twenty who were the "least desirable." The army also agreed to furnish a small contingent of soldiers led by Lieutenant Joseph Morrison. When one sailor fell to his death and four others had to be taken for medical treatment, Smith managed to replace them with five convalescents recruited from the hospital. Macdonough further assisted by transferring sixteen men from the *Montgomery*. The *Eagle* also received twenty-one additional soldiers to serve as acting marines.[38]

Finally in early September, Smith convinced the army's commanding officer to permit him to recruit military prisoners. Undergoing "punishment for various offenses," the forty inmates were "all at work with ball and chain, digging trenches in a kind of red loam." When the lieutenant told the bedraggled prisoners that he "had come to take them to the *Eagle* to fight," they were "delighted at the prospect." After being scrubbed, having their hair cut, trimming their beards, and receiving uniforms, the men were drilled by Smith at the guns "morning and night until the fight came off."[39]

As construction on the *Eagle* continued, Macdonough trained and drilled his other crews. Although lacking experienced sailors, he enjoyed the advantage of time to train his men. During the summer of 1814, he constantly drilled the crews of the *Saratoga*, *Preble*, and

Ticonderoga so that they learned how to sail their ships and operate their guns. Even in the case of the *Eagle*, which did not sail until August 21, Macdonough had several critical weeks to work up the crew. The commander himself prepared an order of battle as well as an order of anchorage for his squadron and produced three hundred detailed numerical signals to be used by his ships. With rumors about British forces and their intentions increasing, Macdonough tried to determine the exact strength of the enemy naval force. At one point he sent an officer disguised as a civilian to accompany Eleazer Williams on one of his spying missions north of the border. By August 29, Williams had been able to help Macdonough's thorough battle preparations by reporting the caliber of each British gun, a development that pleased the navy man, who up until that time had "been somewhat troubled in not knowing the metal of the enemy's naval guns."[40]

While naval construction hurried along at Vergennes and Isle-aux-Noix, the Champlain Valley remained a secondary military theater. Wilkinson had been replaced by Major General George Izard, who assumed command on May 1. The thirty-seven-year-old Izard was a well-connected, promising and ambitious officer. His father had been a delegate to the Continental Congress and a senator from South Carolina. His mother was the niece of New York governor. Educated at military academies in Europe, Izard had graduated from the College of Philadelphia. Commissioned in 1797, he served as an aide-de-camp to army general Alexander Hamilton and as a secretary to his own brother-in-law, the U.S. minister to Portugal. He left the army during President Jefferson's military cutbacks but returned to fight in 1812. As an ambitious officer, Izard hoped that 1814 would bring him the military recognition that he, like many others, sought.

Izard's second in command was Brigadier General Alexander Macomb, another talented young officer. The thirty-two-year-old Macomb had served briefly from 1798 to 1800 before rejoining the service in 1801. After attending West Point, he served as an army engineer for seven years before becoming the army's acting adjutant general. After the War of 1812 began, Macomb entered the artillery branch. He had commanded troops at Sackets Harbor, participated in Dearborn's 1813 York and Niagara campaigns, and accompanied Wilkinson down the Saint Lawrence. With Izard stationed at Plattsburgh, Macomb commanded the troops at Burlington.

Izard's army initially consisted of about 2,000 demoralized, poorly clad, inexperienced, and undisciplined troops who also suffered from poor quality and inadequate provisions. Adding to the general's problems was the quality of his officers, whom Macomb characterized as "totally destitute of military discipline & pride." Some disciplined their troops by privately whipping them, a practice that Izard stopped. In Plattsburgh a considerable amount of tension also existed between the soldiers and rowdy civilians. Fortunately, Izard had several months to restore the morale and discipline of his men.[41]

Meanwhile, by early July, the number of American troops at Chazy and Champlain had swelled to 4,500 while another 600 soldiers worked on fortifications in Plattsburgh. But the center of action in the northern theater continued to be the Niagara frontier in western New York. In July the Americans fought major battles at Chippewa and Lundy's Lane. With more action expected there, Izard recommended to the War Department that he and most of his forces be transferred to western New York.

In the absence of any large military operations, small American and British units conducted periodic incursions back and forth across the border against Odelltown and Champlain. U.S. Army lieutenant colonel Benjamin Forsyth, an aggressive and impatient officer, led several raids, including one in which the Americans seized a British spy at Odelltown and brought him back south. In retaliation the British seized American Elias Hamilton and held him until their man was released. On June 28 Forsyth was mortally wounded as he led a party attempting to lure a British unit into an ambush on Canadian soil. On July 18 a British party of about seventy Canadians and Indians attacked a guard of twenty Americans in Champlain. Although they repulsed the attackers, the Americans lost three dead and three wounded. On August 10 the British lost one of their most resourceful fighters when the Americans mortally wounded Captain Joseph Malloux in an ambush on Canadian soil.[42]

By early August, an actual battle for control of Lake Champlain was brewing. Macdonough was determined to maintain his position on the lake, while the British seemed equally determined to regain control. Shipbuilding efforts in 1814 had furnished each side with a formidable squadron. But the coming battle was not expected to occur until mid-September, when the *Confiance* would be ready, and then it promised to be confined to a naval engagement unlikely to involve land forces. It also seemed likely to be a battle of limited significance because it would involve only the ships of the two small squadrons. Possibly in anticipation of their upcoming clash, Macdonough and his British counterpart, Captain James Fisher, exchanged handwritten notes. Polite and respectful, the messages read as a prelude to a formal challenge in which the two officers would agree to an appointed time for the duel between their respective forces.[43] In Plattsburgh, meanwhile, Izard waited only for War Department approval to move his army entirely from the Champlain Valley. The Americans did not yet recognize the full extent of the British troop buildup or its intended objective. In early August, then, a major invasion of Lake Champlain seemed improbable at best. But the situation was about to change dramatically.

CHAPTER 3

THE BRITISH OCCUPATION OF PLATTSBURGH

By August 1814, the British decision to wage an aggressive war in North America had created a genuine national crisis for the United States. During the summer, the main American offensive along the Niagara frontier had stalled. Americans still controlled Lake Erie and the Detroit frontier, but they had failed to recapture Fort Mackinac and had lost the outpost of Prairie du Chien (in present-day Wisconsin) in July. At the same time, British operations were having a dramatic effect in North America. Under Vice Admiral Cochrane, the British had extended their blockade of the U.S. coast and clamped down on trade with Canada, which had previously been permitted. No longer dependent on American foodstuffs to support its troops in Europe, the British eliminated most of the licenses that permitted that commerce. By the fall, American trade with the Canadas was only 11 percent of what it had been in 1811.[1] The blockade had also isolated the small island of Nantucket, twenty miles off the coast of Massachusetts. Desperate for food and provisions, residents signed a peace treaty that removed them from the war in return for shipping licenses to import food and other necessities from the mainland.

The British had also used their sea power to attack the coast of Maine. On September 1 the navy landed 2,500 troops under Lieutenant General Sir John Sherbrooke, the lieutenant governor of Nova Scotia, who took Castine against light resistance. They then sailed up the Penobscot River to Hampden, where they bottled up and forced Captain Charles Morris to burn the 28-gun USS *Adams*. Subsequently, the British occupied the river to Bangor, took possession of Machias, and issued proclamations by which they took formal possession of the territory, appointed a military governor and a customs official, and offered residents the option of taking a formal loyalty oath or a lesser oath of submission. Britain now controlled one hundred miles of the Maine coast.

With the exception of residents in coastal New England, these actions seemed remote to most Americans until the British also struck the heart of the nation in Chesapeake Bay. As a diversion to support its main army in Canada, the Liverpool government sent a large amphibious force to attack targets in the bay. In part, these strikes were to retaliate for American outrages against civilians, including the May 1814 attack that destroyed all of the homes and mills in Dover on Lake Erie. In June 1814 Governor in Chief Prevost had asked Cochrane "to assist in inflicting that measure of retaliation which shall deter the enemy from a repetition of similar outrages." In response, the admiral issued a general order to "lay waste" to assailable towns along the U.S. coast. Along with this public order, he secretly authorized officers to exempt towns that furnished supplies and to treat others that their forces might occupy with leniency.[2]

In mid-August the British armada of twenty warships and several transports entered Chesapeake Bay. Cochrane dispatched one squadron up the Potomac River toward Alexandria, Virginia, while his main force continued sailing north. Because Washington, D.C., had little strategic or tactical value, officials in the Madison administration assumed that Baltimore, the nation's fourth largest city, or possibly the small accessible port of Annapolis would be their target. As a result, the government took few steps to defend the nation's capital.[3]

The British, however, were headed for Washington. After brushing aside a squadron of gunboats and barges near the mouth of the Patuxent River, 3,400 British troops landed at Benedict, Maryland, and marched uncontested to Bladensburg, near the east branch of the Potomac River. Under the command of Major General Ross, this army was met by inexperienced and poorly organized U.S. forces, which were routed on August 24.

In Washington panic spread quickly as private citizens and public officials fled. President Madison's wife, Dolley, took what precious belongings she could from the Executive Mansion and headed for Virginia. Soon thereafter the president fled by horseback in another direction. Most of his cabinet hurriedly departed in yet another direction toward Frederick, Maryland, where they expected to reassemble. As they entered Washington, the British met virtually no resistance. The invaders set fire to the president's house; the Capitol, which housed the Library of Congress; the Treasury and the building that housed the State and War Departments as well as a number of private homes and other structures. At the Washington Navy Yard, Captain Thomas Tingey followed his orders to burn the facilities and any ships there rather than have them fall into enemy hands.

The next evening the British departed as suddenly as they had come. Following the same route that they had used to advance, the troops embarked on their ships at Benedict on August 30. In the meantime, the smaller detachment had sailed up the Potomac River toward Alexandria. Since the town was undefended, frightened local officials had capitulated to British demands on August 29. Under the harsh terms, the invaders received all local naval supplies and ordnance as well as a rich trove of provisions and foodstuffs from local warehouses. They also seized all private vessels anchored along the river as they headed back down the Potomac.

Within days the two British forces reunited fully intact in lower Chesapeake Bay. The unanswered question was what would be the armada's next destination, for no one thought that the invasion was finished. Baltimore and Annapolis were the obvious next targets, but possibly the enemy would sail out of the Chesapeake and head north for Philadelphia, New York, or Rhode Island. As word of the burning of Washington and the capitulation of Alexandria reached towns up the coast, panic spread quickly. Rumors abounded, but most Americans expected Baltimore to be the next target.

Meanwhile, political opposition had reached an ominous level in Massachusetts.[4] In addition to their opposition to the war, many New England Federalists denounced the administration's wartime embargo against all coastal trade and its failure to protect the coastal communities. The movement to call a special convention of New England states had abated after the embargo was repealed in the spring, but it was reinvigorated by the military events of the summer. With the disastrous news from Washington, Alexandria, Nantucket, and nearby Maine in August, political unrest in Massachusetts grew intense. Many expected that the forces that now occupied coastal Maine would next attack the defenseless city of Boston. A contentious town meeting pressed officials for action. Declaring that he saw "hardly any chance of peace" in the coming months, Massachusetts governor Caleb Strong called the legislature into special session for early October.[5]

In the Champlain Valley the military situation also intensified during August. At the beginning of the month, American forces dominated the area. More than 5,000 troops under the command of Major General Izard were stationed near Plattsburgh, while Master Commandant Macdonough's squadron controlled the lake. Although a naval battle between the British and American forces seemed likely, it promised to be one of limited, local significance.

With a large number of British troops reported to be gathering between Montreal and Lake Champlain, the Americans still did not know the actual intentions of Governor in Chief Prevost, whose secret instructions from the Liverpool government gave him considerable latitude. He was to use the reinforcements being sent from Europe "to commence offensive operations on the Enemy's Frontier before the close of this campaign." While Lord Bathurst's instructions spoke of protecting and defending Canada, they ordered offensive actions. "The object of your operations will be; first, to give immediate protection [to Canada]: secondly, to obtain if possible ultimate security to His Majesty's Possession in America." Accordingly, "the entire destruction of Sacket's Harbor and the Naval Establishment on Lake Erie and Lake Champlain come under the first description," while the "maintenance of Ft. Niagara . . . and the occupation of Detroit and the Michigan Country come under the second." Finally, "should there be any advance position on that part of our frontier which extends towards Lake Champlain, the occupation of which would materially tend to the security of the province, you will if you deem it expedient expel the Enemy from it, and occupy it." These instructions warned Prevost "not [to] expose His Majesty's Forces to being cut off by too extended a line of advance." The British government also pressured him to attack as soon as possible. "If you shall allow the present campaign to close without having taken offensive measures," the government warned, "you will seriously disappoint the expectations of the Prince regent and the country."[6]

When Prevost received these instructions in July, he decided to attack Lake Champlain rather than to strike the Niagara or Detroit frontiers. For him, this was the most logical and feasible decision with only a brief campaign window remaining in 1814. With his reinforcements slow to arrive, it was not until August 17 that Prevost reported all of them having reached Canada.[7] An attack on either Sackets Harbor or Detroit was not yet feasible since the British did not have naval control of either Lake Erie or Lake Ontario with which to support a large invading force. The American navy controlled Lake Erie, and the earliest that the British navy might hope to command Lake Ontario would be mid-October, when the construction of a huge warship, HMS *St. Lawrence*, was expected to be completed.

An offensive against Lake Champlain from Montreal offered positive advantages. Strategically important, the Champlain Valley–Richelieu River corridor between Montreal and the Hudson River offered the shortest and most direct path for Prevost to strike an offensive blow. The operation could be conducted quickly in the short campaigning season remaining in 1814 and would not overextend his invading army. Since this also offered the most direct way for the United States to invade Lower Canada, control of Lake Champlain would immensely strengthen Montreal's security. The rough terrain would also make it virtually impossible for the Americans to outflank or cut off an invading force. And in the unlikely event that a retreat became necessary, the army could depend on a well-secured return route to the city.[8]

An invasion directed at Lake Champlain also solved the challenge of sustaining a large army in the wilderness. Prevost's army daily consumed forty-five tons of food and supplies. In addition to the large stockpile of material accumulated twenty miles north of the border at Chambly, Prevost could count on the support of American smugglers. In August he estimated that "two thirds of the army are supplied with beef by American contractors, principally of Vermont and New York." This illegal practice frustrated U.S. commanders. Macdonough noted, "The supplying of the enemy by many citizens of Vermont is in daily practice." Izard also complained that "droves of cattle are continually passing from the northern parts of this state [Vermont] into Canada for the British." He noted that on "the eastern side of Lake Champlain the high roads are insufficient for the cattle pouring into Canada. Like herds of buffalo they press through the forests, making paths for themselves. Were it not for these supplies, the British forces in Canada would soon be suffering from famine."[9]

Americans did not know Prevost's instructions or his intentions, but it was public knowledge that thousands of additional troops were being sent to Canada. In northern New York Macdonough and Izard also received reports from Eleazer Williams's rangers and other sources that a British-troop buildup was underway across the border from Lake Champlain. In fact, more than 10,000 soldiers were camped at Odelltown and Chambly by the third week of August.

Prevost attempted to disguise his intention and divert American attention by sending 3,000 reinforcements up the Saint Lawrence River to Lake Ontario. As a result, although their anxiety grew, American officials were slow to recognize the full extent of the British buildup south of Montreal or that their objective would be Lake Champlain, not Lake Ontario.[10]

Across the border, General Izard prepared to withdraw 4,000 of his troops in order to get his men into the thick of the combat in western New York. His July 19 recommendation for this action to the War Department crossed en route with a July 27 letter from Secretary of War Armstrong ordering Izard to move most of his troops west from Plattsburgh. But by the time the general finally received this order on August 11, it had become apparent that a British offensive against Lake Champlain was likely. Izard immediately requested that his instructions be reversed and that his army remain near Plattsburgh, predicting that otherwise the American fortifications on Cumberland Head and in Plattsburgh "will in less than three days after my departure be in the possession of the enemy." His plans astonished and frustrated Williams, who reported that Macdonough was also "greatly chagrined at the intentions of the government." Nine days later Izard confirmed that he would obey orders and move his troops, but "I must not be responsible for the consequences of abandoning my present strong position. . . . Major-Gen'l Brisbane commands at Odeltown, he is said to have between 3 & 6,000 men with him; at Chambly are stated to be about 4,000." He then prepared to move his army after receiving no response from the War Department.[11]

Prevost's basic plan was direct and cautious. From its base just north of the border, his army would move to capture Plattsburgh while the British naval squadron at Isle-aux-Noix seized control of Lake Champlain. Prevost selected the New York shore as his invasion route. "Vermont has shown a disinclination to the war, and, as it is sending in specie and provisions," he wrote on August 5 to London, "I will confine offensive operations to the west side of Lake Champlain." Once he occupied Plattsburgh, Prevost intended to send a brigade to destroy the U.S. naval base at Vergennes and other targets around the lake.[12] While planning the invasion in Montreal, he explained the precise objective of the offensive to his daughter, Ann, wrote, "The Principal object of the expedition, as I afterwards understood, was the destruction of the American Dock

Yard at Vincennes [*sic*] on the opposite side of the Lake—and the capture of Plattsburg would be merely the first service effected by the Expedition on its way to an ulterior object." In this way Prevost planned to secure a solid foothold on American soil without the risk of having his army cut off from behind.[13]

Since naval control of the lake was critical to the invasion, Prevost planned a joint operation. "Of course," his daughter later explained, "it was first of all most necessary that the American Squadron should be defeated, and our command of the Lake quite established." While the small American navy could not prevent his army from marching along the lake and capturing Plattsburgh, Prevost understood that the primitive roads and rough, wooded terrain made control of the water essential. As his quartermaster general, Major General William Robinson, noted: "The roads are worse than you can imagine and many of our wagons are broken down— The road through the woods at Beatville [Beekmantown] is impassable therefore our only dependence is upon water communication." Accordingly, the American squadron would have to be destroyed. If some ships managed to flee from an initial battle, they would be hunted down and destroyed later.[14]

At Chambly, twenty miles south of Montreal and twenty miles north of the U.S. border, the British had accumulated a large stockpile of supplies and provisions. By mid-August, Prevost concentrated in the area fourteen battalions of infantry, including six battalions of elite veterans from the Duke of Wellington's Iberian campaigns. Although Major General Francis Baron de Rottenburg commanded this army, its three brigades would be led by three of Wellington's finest combat officers: Major Generals Frederick Phillipe Robinson, Thomas Brisbane, and Manley Power. All were tough, aggressive, and seasoned commanders who had fought successfully in Europe and expected similar results in North America.[15]

Despite the strength of Prevost's new army and its leadership, morale remained an issue. The veterans and their officers who had served in Europe resented being sent to fight a secondary colonial war. They would have much preferred to remain in Europe as an army of occupation or to be sent home to England on leave. Now that they were in the wilderness of North America, desertion became a temptation for disillusioned soldiers. Prevost understood this threat and planned accordingly for a quick campaign that would not become bogged down or linger on American soil. The veteran officers also resented Prevost and his two major generals, Edward Baynes and Baron de Rottenburg, who outranked all of their generals, even though neither of them had extensive combat experience. In comparison to their legendary former commander, the Duke of Wellington, they also found Prevost to be an officious and petty commander who was not even of British descent. For example, in the field Wellington had allowed considerable latitude with respect to the dress of his officers. Once in Canada, however, Prevost rankled them by issuing a general order directing his officers to adhere strictly to uniform regulations.[16]

At Isle-aux-Noix, the British assembled a small but formidable squadron, consisting of the 16-gun *Linnet*, the 11-gun *Chub*, the 11-gun *Finch*, and twelve gunboats carrying 1 or 2 guns each. (The *Chub* and the *Finch* were the two sloops captured from the Americans the previous year.) These vessels were not superior to the American fleet, but the British expected to tip the balance of naval power with the 37-gun *Confiance*. In addition to being considerably larger than any American ship, the *Confiance* would carry twenty-seven 24-pound long guns, which theoretically made it unbeatable from a range of more than 1,000 yards since the largest U.S. ship, the 26-gun *Saratoga*, carried only eight 24-pounders. Although construction lagged, the *Confiance* was nearing completion by mid-August and was expected to be fully operational by mid-September.

Prevost was helped immensely by what seemed to be a stroke of extraordinary good fortune. On August 27, after delaying as long as he could, General Izard and 4,000 of his regulars began to leave the Plattsburgh area. Two days later they had all departed. In Plattsburgh Williams reported "great alarm among the citizens of this place. . . . It is not only gloomy, but distressing, to see the poor taking their all upon their backs and flying from their peaceful abodes."[17]

Brigadier General Macomb was now left behind in Plattsburgh with more than 3,000 regulars and volunteers, but roughly 1,400 were unavailable for duty because they were sick or had earlier been assigned to duty on Macdonough's ships. The core of Macomb's forces consisted of six regiments totaling 1,770 men, supplemented by 700 New York militia troops. As it became apparent that an invasion was imminent, the general made the critical decision to stand and fight even though Plattsburgh itself contained little of value. A contemporary observer noted that the village "is overrun with grog shops and taverns . . . all looks vulgar. . . . The streets are very dirty;

on the whole it's a pretty dirty place." Moreover, as Plattsburgh was poorly fortified, Macomb would be at a huge defensive disadvantage. Although estimates vary, the invading force consisted of more than 10,000 troops, about 8,300 of whom reached Plattsburgh, while another 2,000 guarded communications back into Canada. The British soldiers were also well-supplied and capably led veterans. Given this numerical imbalance, some local leaders and even some of Macomb's officers advised the general that he abandon Plattsburgh and retreat rather than risk having the village destroyed and his army annihilated by the superior enemy force.[18]

On September 1 Macomb described his seemingly hopeless situation to the War Department. He declared "everything in a state of disorganization—works unfinished & a garrison of a few efficient men and a sick list of one thousand. . . . Happen what will you may rely that the garrison will do its utmost." While the general contemplated this situation, fear and panic spread in Plattsburgh. "The people are all frighten'd nearly out—out, did I say? Rather into their *wits*—if they have any—moving everything off—under the expectation that all will be burnt or destroyed," observed U.S. Army surgeon Dr. William Beaumont. "Poor souls, many of them, love & uphold the British—censure & condemn our own Government—complaining they have no protection—neither will they take up arms to defend themselves—Indeed I pity their depravity—but don't care much for their losses—if they should maintain any."[19]

A determined Macomb, however, immediately called for intelligence and assistance. He was now receiving reports every ten hours from the American spy Eleazer Williams and his rangers. He also appealed for assistance from the militias of New York and Vermont. Volunteers quickly began to flow to Plattsburgh in a steady stream. Within days, hundreds of men had appeared. Among them was a small company of local teenagers who were not old enough to enlist but volunteered anyway on September 3. Their services were accepted only when militia captain Martin Aikin agreed to sponsor them. Known as Aikin's Rifle Company, this group of about twenty eager boys played an important role in scouting and harassing the enemy. Williams found them "not only useful watching our front line, but they are brave and daring in skirmishing with the enemy." On one occasion three of them crossed the river to observe the British and retrieve supplies known to be hidden in a barn. When enemy soldiers discovered and fired on them, the three were fortunate to escape back across the river. "There is no corps more useful and watchful," claimed Williams, "than the one under the command of Captain Aikin and Lieut. Flagg."[20]

On September 5 Macomb issued a general order to his officers and men. "The eyes of America are on us. . . . Fortune always follows the brave. . . . [T]he General thinks it is his duty to detail, that every man may know and do his duty."[21] He also knew that his small force would not be able to outmaneuver the oncoming British army. Instead, he would defend Plattsburgh by forcing the invaders to displace the Americans from several small fortifications. For this operation, Macomb was particularly well qualified as one of the first officers trained at West Point, where the curriculum emphasized engineering. Before the war, he had not served in the infantry or in the dragoons but as an engineering officer whose responsibility prior to the War of 1812 was to supervise the construction of various defensive fortifications. Once hostilities began, Macomb moved to the artillery, where he quickly distinguished himself.

The general scrambled to strengthen three small forts and two blockhouses in Plattsburgh. Fortunately, Izard had left behind Major Joseph Totten, an engineer, to assist. The village was divided by the Saranac River, which runs in a northeastern direction before emptying into Cumberland Bay on Lake Champlain. It helped form a sort of small peninsula, bounded on the north and west by the river and on the east by the bay. South of the Saranac, Macomb strengthened Forts Scott, Moreau, and Brown as well as two blockhouses in order to make his stand. As the work proceeded, the general himself worked side by side with his soldiers. At one point, when Williams returned from one of his missions to report, he found the "General . . . marching with his men, with a heavy pine stick on his shoulders, which had so painted him with its black coal, that I hardly recognized him."[22] Macomb withdrew a small detachment of troops from Cumberland Head in an effort to strengthen his position in town. Since the chosen area was adjacent to the lake, Macomb and Macdonough agreed to deploy the American naval forces close enough to shore to furnish additional fire support.

On September 1 Macdonough moved his squadron from a position north of Cumberland Head into Cumberland Bay. This force consisted of the ten gunboats as well as the 7-gun *Preble* and the three ships built in 1814: the 17-gun *Ticonderoga*, the 26-gun *Saratoga*, and the 20-gun *Eagle*. The sloops *President* and

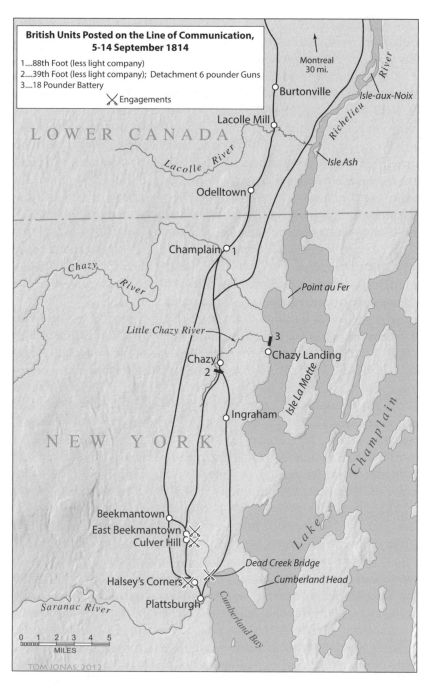

Montgomery had been assigned to transport duty, a decision that allowed Macdonough to transfer some seamen to his warships. Still, the American fleet remained short of manpower. As they awaited the invaders, Macdonough and Macomb communicated well and agreed on their objective: to combine their land and naval forces to defend Plattsburgh. Macdonough clearly understood that he needed both to employ his squadron to prevent the British from surrounding Macomb's army in Plattsburgh and to somehow maintain U.S. naval supremacy on the lake.[23] Although they had their differences, the two commanders worked well together to achieve their common objective. In this respect their professional relationship exhibited a sharp contrast to that of many of their older, prideful, ego-driven counterparts who refused to cooperate to achieve a critical goal—in particular, Wilkinson and Hampton in 1813.

That same day the British made an unexpected and fateful command change when Captain George Downie arrived to replace Captain Fisher and take charge of the British squadron. Several months earlier, Commodore Yeo had sent Fisher to take command at Isle-aux-Noix because he believed that Captain Pring was too junior an officer to supervise construction of the new frigate there. Now Fisher was being abruptly replaced without any apparent compelling reason. Although they respected each other, apparently there was some tension between Yeo and Fisher. The commodore might have been miffed by the slow construction of the warship, or possibly he resented the fact that Fisher and Prevost became close associates during the summer of 1814, when they occasionally dined and talked at length at the governor's residence in Montreal. In an apparent unsuccessful attempt to smooth their differences, Fisher named the new frigate *Confiance* in recognition of a vessel of the same name on which Yeo had served in the Mediterranean.[24]

Downie was an accomplished commander, but Yeo's decision was highly questionable. With Prevost's invasion already underway, the timing of the captain's arrival was terrible. Downie had combat experience in European and Mediterranean waters, but he had never sailed on or even seen Lake Champlain. He had no firsthand knowledge of the winds, currents, or island shoals and would literally have no time to gain such knowledge of the waters on which he would fight. Moreover, Downie was a stranger to the officers and men of the squadron. Other than his first lieutenant, James Robertson, the captain did not know and had never served with any of them.

At Isle-aux-Noix the officers and men were a mixed bag. The *Chub* and the *Finch* already had their crews. Captain Pring knew the waters of the lake well and in 1814 had trained a disciplined crew on the *Linnet*. But the most important ship, the *Confiance*, was a problem. Its crew was late to arrive and consisted of a combination of landsmen or sailors collected from other warships or transports. Although a few volunteers were excellent seamen, most were not, having been sent to Isle-aux-Noix either against their wishes or because they were in some disgrace. According to Pring, the *Confiance* had an "unorganized crew, comprised of several Drafts of Men, who had recently arrived from different ships at Quebec, many of whom only joined the day before, and were totally unknown either to the Officers or to each other."[25]

The timing of Downie's appointment also presented an operational problem. Since the invasion had already begun when he arrived, he would not have an opportunity to earn the confidence and trust of his officers or to develop a strong sense of unit cohesion among his crews. Moreover, although he and Prevost had met in Montreal before they arrived at Isle-aux-Noix, by the time Downie assumed command on September 3, the governor in chief and his army had already crossed the border into New York. In the few days before the naval battle, the two commanders communicated only through their subordinates or brief written messages. Since Prevost had not prepared a written battle plan, the likelihood for a misunderstanding was strong.

Once he took command, Downie faced a daunting task. Three of his ships were prepared and ready for battle, but the *Confiance* was not. It had been launched on August 25, but outfitters and carpenters still swarmed the decks. Most of the crew did not embark until September 5, the last arriving on the ninth. There were also equipment problems. Since the magazine was not finished, ordnance had to be towed in small boats behind the frigate when it entered the lake. Most of the gunlocks had not arrived yet, forcing the men to adapt temporary locks for the long guns from carronade locks. In fact, on the day he took command, Downie sent a letter to the captain of HMS *Junon*, then at Quebec, asking to borrow temporarily "the whole of the *Junon*'s Locks, even for the time she may remain at Quebec." According to the ship's master, once fitted the "guns in general worked very heavy, owing to the decks being rough-scraped and [with] a quantity of Pitch on them."[26]

Initially, as the British began their invasion on August 31, these issues seemed not to matter. First across the border were the troops commanded by General Brisbane. Then on September 1 Prevost crossed into New York, distributing and posting a public proclamation that assured "peaceable and unoffending inhabitants" that they could expect "kind usage and generous treatment." His Majesty's arms were directed "against the government of the United States by whom this unjust and unprovoked war has been declared and against those who support it, either openly or secretly."[27]

Prevost's advance went well, even though the terrain on the western shore of Lake Champlain was heavily wooded, rough, and impassable except for primitive roads from north to south. The British secured the north end of the lake and captured Isle La Motte near the mouth of the Little Chazy River, where Prevost intended to land his transports. The army reached the town of Chazy and camped in the vicinity. It then marched to the tiny village of Beekmantown and on September 5 marched the final few miles to Plattsburgh in two columns. The left column was closer to the lake and would enter the town over the Dead Creek Bridge near its northeastern edge. Meanwhile, slightly inland, the right column marched south farther inland.

On September 6 the progress of the British right was slowed by trees that the Americans had felled across the road and by sporadic opposition from 700 New York militiamen, volunteers such as Aikin's Rifle Company and a small detachment of regulars led by Major John Wool. Skirmishes occurred, and snipers killed several British officers. Still, the resistance proved ineffective. Most of the militiamen fled from the British, and the American regulars continually had to fall back rather than be overtaken. The British never deployed their units and continued to march in unbroken columns. The left column marched unchallenged until it reached Dead Creek Bridge. After the troops broke through a barrier there, waiting U.S. gunboats fired on them until British artillery returned fire and dispersed the American vessels.[28]

As they entered Plattsburgh, the two columns reunited. Scattered but sharp resistance from small American detachments erupted, but by the end of the day, the British occupied the village to the edge of the Saranac. As the Americans retreated across the upper and lower bridges on the river, Macomb ordered them to remove the deck planking from the spans. Although estimates vary widely, the

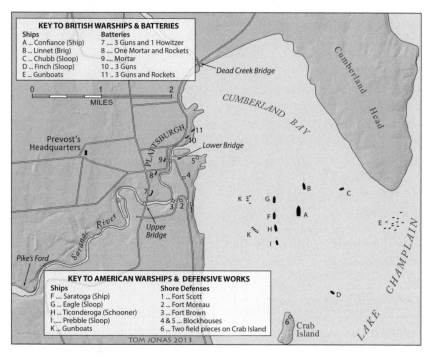

KEY TO BRITISH WARSHIPS & BATTERIES

Ships	Batteries
A ... Confiance (Ship)	7 .... 3 Guns and 1 Howitzer
B ... Linnet (Brig)	8 .... One Mortar and Rockets
C ... Chubb (Sloop)	9 .... Mortar
D ... Finch (Sloop)	10 ... 3 Guns
E ... Gunboats	11 .. 3 Guns and Rockets

KEY TO AMERICAN WARSHIPS & DEFENSIVE WORKS

Ships	Shore Defenses
F .... Saratoga (Ship)	1 ... Fort Scott
G ... Eagle (Sloop)	2 ... Fort Moreau
H .... Ticonderoga (Schooner)	3 ... Fort Brown
I .... Prebble (Sloop)	4 & 5 ... Blockhouses
K ... Gunboats	6 ... Two field pieces on Crab Island

TOM JONAS 2013

British and American Positions around Plattsburgh. Map by Tom Jonas. From Grodzinski, *Defender of Canada*, 177. Used by permission.

British had suffered about two hundred killed and wounded, while the Americans lost about fifty. An estimated one hundred soldiers had deserted during the march, but Major General Mooers reported that many of his seven hundred New York militiamen had "fled at the first approach of the enemy, and afterwards basely disbanded themselves and returned home; thereby disgracing themselves, and furnishing to their fellow-soldiers an example of all that brave men detest and abhor."[29]

By the morning of September 7, the battle lines had been drawn in Plattsburgh as sporadic skirmishing continued and casualties rose. The British now occupied the town, where Prevost established his headquarters. His force at hand consisted of 8,072 officers and men fit for duty. Of these, 2,625 officers and men had served in Wellington's forces in Spain. The British soon established four batteries. By September 11, Prevost also had twenty-five field pieces available. He had sent for four additional guns from Isle-aux-Noix, but they did not arrive in time for the coming battle.[30]

The Americans had deployed themselves south of the Saranac River on the peninsula between the river and Cumberland Bay. They had also taken control of a key ford, known as Pike's Ford, three miles west up the river. American forces in town manned the two blockhouses and Forts Brown, Moreau, and Scott. To combat British snipers in buildings close to the river, Macomb shelled and fired hot shot into the enemy positions, thereby destroying fifteen private buildings and the courthouse. News of Prevost's invasion had spurred hundreds of volunteers from Vermont to scurry across the lake to Plattsburgh as quickly as possible. Since he had no time to drill or train them, Macomb did his best to organize and inspire the many newcomers.[31]

In the several days before the battle, both sides strengthened their positions. The Americans feverishly dug trenches around their fortifications, while the British constructed gun positions north of the river. Since the town had been shelled and various buildings still smoldered, the smoke sheltered this activity from American view and gunfire. Exchanges of gunfire and skirmishes occurred daily. On the night of September 9, an American detachment of fifty men led by Captain George McGlassin conducted a particularly audacious raid on a British battery near Fort Brown. Once across the river, the group managed to frighten and drive off a British work party and protecting force of three hundred men by approaching in a noisy manner from two directions. The Americans then spiked the battery's guns and returned to their base without casualties.

Macomb attempted to deceive Prevost into thinking that the American force was much larger than it actually was by moving large numbers of men from fort to fort in Plattsburgh and parading them openly when changing the guard at each. The general also arranged for a counterfeit letter, stating that Vermont governor Martin Chittenden was on his way with 10,000 men, to fall into British hands. And he managed for suspected spies to overhear a conversation about Izard's army returning to Plattsburgh. Since the British knew of Pike's Ford from their raid on the town the previous year, Macomb ordered that the roads between the ford and the village be observed and obstructed by men working in the dense forest under the cover of darkness.[32]

The effect of these efforts to strengthen the fortifications and to mislead Prevost is unclear. In such primitive wilderness conditions, military commanders routinely had to deal with inaccurate reports and false intelligence before a major battle. But Macomb's efforts sent a clear message that while the British army greatly outnumbered their opponents, the American force was considerably larger than it had been just a week earlier. Moreover, whatever its numerical disadvantage, these were men who intended to stand and fight stubbornly at Plattsburgh. By nature and by experience, Prevost was a cautious and tentative commander, not an audacious and aggressive warrior. As a result, these actions certainly gave him pause on the eve of the battle.

With the heavy guns in place by September 9, the British were now able to threaten Macdonough's anchored ships in Cumberland Bay and to shell the forts across the Saranac. This development changed the character of the coming battle. Macdonough was forced to move his entire squadron farther away from shore to the southeast. Now out of range of British artillery, Macdonough's vessels were also unable to aid Macomb's forts with supporting fire against the enemy gun positions. The British artillery had thus ensured that the upcoming contest would consist of two separate engagements: one between land forces on shore and the other between the two navies on the lake. Given the overwhelming numerical advantages of the invaders on land and their confident expectation that their squadron would either destroy or scatter the American warships, a decisive British victory seemed certain.[33]

Macdonough himself had decided to deploy his entire fleet in Cumberland Bay, out of range of the British shore batteries but carefully anchored for battle. His greatest concern was the 37-gun HMS *Confiance*, which far exceeded the destructive power of his own flagship. The long guns of the frigate gave the British an overwhelming advantage over the carronades of the 26-gun USS *Saratoga* at long range on the open lake. But if the British squadron could be forced to fight in the bay, several factors would lessen its advantage. Roughly two miles wide, Cumberland Bay was a confined arena. Its waters were capricious, with shoals extending from the shore. The wind in the bay was also tricky and unpredictable. Moreover, the British would need a brisk wind from the north to sail down the lake, but once they rounded Cumberland Head, that wind would likely create problems. The land mass of Cumberland Head tended to break up a north wind to create a baffling breeze in the bay. Such a fluttering wind would make it difficult for the British ships to maneuver. In contrast, the American ships would fight from stationary, anchored positions, which meant that their inexperienced crews could concentrate solely on fighting their guns rather than maneuvering their vessels. Macdonough was a student of naval history who knew that the Royal Navy had won decisive victories by attacking anchored enemy fleets at Copenhagen and on the Nile. Given their great confidence, British commanders were unlikely to avoid engaging the American squadron at anchor in Cumberland Bay.[34]

Macdonough positioned his ships in a line from northeast to southwest in the bay. The *Eagle* was the northernmost unit, followed by the *Saratoga* (Macdonough's flagship), then the *Ticonderoga*, and finally the *Preble*. At the north end of the American line, it would be difficult if not impossible for British ships to sail around or flank the *Eagle*. At the southern end of the line, shoals extending from Crab Island would make it equally difficult for the British to flank the *Preble*.

In anchoring his ships, Macdonough employed a standard naval practice of the day that proved decisive during the battle. In confined anchorages, naval commanders often used multiple, secured anchors. With two main anchors and supporting kedge anchors secured by spring lines on each side of its bow and stern, a ship could be repositioned in place or turned from end to end by releasing one of the anchors and drawing in the spring lines of others, a procedure was known as "winding the ship." Although not used in naval combat on the open seas, winding could be invaluable for an anchored squadron in a confined combat area. By winding his ship, a commander could bring an entire fresh broadside of guns from one side into action if the guns from the other side became disabled.[35]

Macdonough had planned well and prepared thoroughly, but to a considerable extent his success would depend on the willingness of his unproven men to execute his orders under the terrifying conditions of naval combat. Joseph H. Dulles, a recent graduate of Yale College, visited Lake Champlain in August 1814 and was impressed with the naval commander when they dined on the *Saratoga*. He described Macdonough as having a "light and agile frame, easy and graceful in his manners, with an expressive countenance, remarkably placid." The master commandant was a "very polite" man who spoke "very little" and never used "any profane language." Dulles also noted that the "officers put the most unbounded confidence in his bravery and prudence." When the observer asked one midshipman about the coming battle, the young man answered, "We know the British force to be superior to ours, but we will do our duty."[36]

By September 8, Prevost was prepared to attack, but the navy was yet to be seen. While the other ships of the British squadron waited, feverish work continued on the *Confiance*. After being towed into the lake, the frigate finally joined the fleet on September 8, but it was still not battle ready. Its guns were not yet fully equipped, and the gun crews went to their stations only that day. It was not until the ninth that the ship's battery was exercised for the first time.

Although Downie assured Prevost on September 7 that he would be ready for combat "the moment I can put this ship in a state for action," an uncharacteristically impatient Prevost pressed for an immediate sortie. "I only wait your arrival to proceed against General Macomb's last position," he wrote on September 8. The same day a testy Downie replied, "I stated to you that the ship was not ready—she is not ready now, and until she is ready, it is my duty not to hazard the Squadron before an Enemy who will be superior in Force." The next day Prevost informed the captain that having postponed his own assault, he "need not dwell with you on the evils resulting to both Services from delay."[37]

Always a cautious commander, Prevost had now grown impatient because of the opportunity presenting itself at Plattsburgh. According to Major General Robinson, the governor in chief pressured Downie because "a *golden opportunity* presented itself for totally annihilating the enemy flotilla, and gaining the superiority of the Lakes for the war."[38] With an inferior U.S. force confronting Prevost in the town, Macdonough's naval squadron rested at anchor in the bay. Here, then, was a rare chance for the British to smash an American army onshore while destroying an American fleet anchored conveniently offshore. On September 8 Prevost had informed Downie that the navy's role in the operation "will be to destroy or to Capture the Enemy's Squadron, if it should wait for a contest . . . , but if it should run away and get out of your reach, we must meet here to consult on Ulterior movements."[39] Now, unless the captain moved quickly, the chance for a decisive combined victory might be lost.

Although the *Confiance* was still not completely prepared, Downie decided to sail on September 10, though strong winds from the south prevented his doing so. A frustrated Prevost informed him that the troops had been waiting since six o'clock that morning but were unable to storm the enemy's position because his warships had not appeared. Acknowledging his disappointment at the "unfortunate change of wind," a testy Prevost added that he "shall rejoice to learn that my reasonable expectations have been frustrated by no other cause." Finally, aided by brisk and favorable northeastern winds, the British squadron set sail before dawn on Sunday, September 11.[40]

The general expectation that morning was that the invaders were about to score a clear victory. The Americans would prove to be no match for the British veterans in Plattsburgh or the British naval force on Lake Champlain. The British were about to seize naval control of the lake and overrun the defenders in the village. Although the details of the military situation were not then known beyond Plattsburgh, a British victory was also confidently anticipated in Canada, London, and Ghent as well as by many in the United States.

Commodore Thomas Macdonough (ca. 1815/18), by Gilbert Stuart. Oil on wood, 28 9/16 x 35 in. (72.5 x 58.6 cm). Courtesy National Gallery of Art, Washington, D.C., Andrew W. Mellon Collection, 1942.8.1

Alexander Macomb (1809), by Charles Balthazar Julien Févret de Saint Mémin. Engraving on paper. Courtesy National Portrait Gallery, Smithsonian Institution; gift of Mr. and Mrs. Paul Mellon.

Sir George Prevost, by Samuel William Reynolds. National Archives of Canada, C-6152. Courtesy of Canadian Heritage Gallery, www.canadianheritage.ca, item 10233.

The Battle of Lake Champlain (1894), by Julian Davidson. War of 1812
Museum, Battle of Plattsburgh Association. Courtesy of the Battle of Lake
Champlain Association.

A Hundred Years Peace: The Signature of the Treaty of Ghent (1914), lithograph of painting by A. Forestier. Metropolitan Toronto Reference Library, J. Ross Robertson Collection, T15457. Courtesy of Canadian Heritage Gallery, www.canadianheritage.ca, item 20020.

CHAPTER 4

THE BATTLE OF LAKE CHAMPLAIN, SEPTEMBER 11, 1814

The British squadron finally had set sail for Plattsburgh. Unlike recent days, the early morning of September 11 was bright and sunny. The artificers and riggers remained at work on the *Confiance* and would not leave the ship until just before the fighting began. Captain Downie expected that once his ships attacked the American squadron anchored in Cumberland Bay, Governor in Chief Prevost's land forces would simultaneously assault the American defenders on shore. As a signal to prepare for the joint assault, Downie scaled his guns, or fired blank shots, as he approached Cumberland Head shortly after 5:00 A.M. Both the British and Americans on board their respective ships on either side of Cumberland Head were able to see the mast heads of their opponent vessels. Shortly thereafter, all of the British commanders met to receive their final orders from Downie.[1]

As he approached the tip of Cumberland Head, Downie left his flagship to reconnoiter the American position in a small boat. In addition to the line of principal U.S. warships, he also noted that six larger galleys and four smaller gunboats were stationed to its west. The captain then returned to his flagship to give his crew a final message. "There are the Enemy's Ships," he declared, "our Army are to storm the Enemy works at the moment we engage, and mind don't let us be behind." The crew cheered their captain and returned to their stations.[2] With rumors of the impending battle widespread, numerous residents and civilians waited on Cumberland Head to witness history firsthand. On the lake British and Canadian civilians on a small vessel watched at a safe distance from the warships.

Downie planned an aggressive attack to secure a decisive victory. He decided not to employ his four warships individually to engage each of their four American counterparts. Instead, in classic British fashion, he intended to concentrate his force on the northern end, or van, of the U.S. line. The combined 64 guns of the HMS *Confiance*, the HMS *Linnet,* and the HMS *Chub* would overwhelm the two most powerful enemy ships, the 20-gun USS *Eagle* and the 26-gun USS *Saratoga.* Downie planned to sail the *Confiance* to the head of the American line, fire a double-shotted starboard broadside at the *Eagle,* and then anchor "athwart Bows of the *Saratoga.*" With its port guns, the *Confiance* would then engage the smaller *Saratoga.* Closely accompanying the *Confiance,* the *Linnet* and the *Chub* would anchor and attack the *Eagle.* Downie directed his eleven gunboats to approach with the "greatest expedition, fire once, and then board the [USS] *Ticonderoga,*" while HMS *Finch* supported them and attacked the weakest of the enemy ships, the 7-gun USS *Preble.* Once the *Saratoga* and the *Eagle* had surrendered or been destroyed, the full squadron would finish off *Ticonderoga* and *Preble.*[3]

As Downie's ships moved into Cumberland Bay about eight o'clock, the two fleets seemed evenly balanced. The four British warships and eleven gunboats totaled just over 2,400 tons and carried 917 men, while the four American warships and ten gunboats totaled 2,224 tons and carried 820 men. The British ships carried more than 90 guns with a total metal weight of 1,864 pounds, while the American ships had 86 guns with a total metal weight of 2,033 pounds. Yet there was a considerable difference in gun type. The British long guns totaled 1,128 pounds of throw-weight to only 759 pounds for the Americans, but the latter had an advantage of 1,274 pounds to Britain's 736 pounds of throw-weight in carronades. With its 37 guns, the 1,200-ton *Confiance* had considerable superiority over the smaller 734-ton *Saratoga,* which carried only 26 guns. The frigate had its greatest advantage at a range of more than 1,000 yards because it carried twenty-seven 24-pound long guns, while the *Saratoga* carried only eight 24-pounders. Yet at a range of less than 500 yards, the advantage shifted because the *Saratoga* carried eighteen carronades, while the *Confiance* carried only ten such guns.[4] Sometimes called smashers, carronades were particularly destructive at a close range. Thus, British and American warships typically carried a combination of both long guns and carronades.

Although both squadrons struggled with the quality and experience of their crews, the British seemed to have a distinct advantage in its seasoned and confident commander. The thirty-six-year-old Downie had entered the Royal Navy in the 1790s and been promoted to lieutenant in 1802, having been commended twice for his conduct in combat. In 1805 his commander praised Downie as "a most

The Naval Squadrons at the Battle of Lake Champlain, September 11, 1814

Ship (Commander)	Tons	Crew	Guns	
AMERICAN FORCE				
Ship *Saratoga* (Macdonough)	734	210	26	
Brig *Eagle* (Henley)	480	120	20	
Schooner *Ticonderoga* (Cassin)	350	110	17	
Sloop *Preble* (Budd)	80	30	7	
6 Gunboats	420	226	12	(2 each)
4 Gunboats	160	104	4	(1 each)
Total	**2,224**	**820**	**86**	
BRITISH FORCE				
Frigate *Confiance* (Downie)	1,200	300	37	
Brig *Linnet* (Pring)	350	120	16	
Sloop *Chub* (McGhie)	112	40	11	
Sloop *Finch* (Hicks)	110	40	11	
5 Gunboats	350		10	(2 each)
7 Gunboats	280	417	7	(1 each)
Total	**2,402**	**917**	**92**	

Data compiled from the following: Everest, *War of 1812 in the Champlain Valley*, 205; Macdonough, *Life of Commodore Thomas Macdonough*, 120, 121; Wood, *Select British Documents of the Canadian War of 1812*, 3(1):366, 373.

zealous officer" for his role in attacking and cutting out a Spanish ordnance vessel loaded with powder at Saint Pedro. After an attack in 1808 that captured several Turkish warships, his commander recommended him for promotion as an officer of "merit, ability and experience." As commander of the 18-gun-brig HMS *Royalist*, Downie had captured several French privateers in 1810 and 1811. Promoted to post captain, he was sent to North America in 1814. After being placed in the command of HMS *Montreal*, Downie was abruptly sent to Isle-aux-Noix in August to assume command of British naval forces there. In this new assignment he was accompanied by an experienced first lieutenant, James Robertson, both related to and respected by his commander.[5]

Downie's second in command, Captain Daniel Pring of HMS *Linnet*, was only twenty-six years old but was already an experienced and resourceful officer. Since being assigned to the Isle-aux-Noix base, Pring had led several raids and knew the waters of northern Lake Champlain well. The commander of the *Finch*, twenty-seven-year-old Lieutenant William Hicks, had joined the British navy in 1805 and had seen action on several warships. On Lake Champlain he had participated in the British raid on Plattsburgh in 1813 and the assault on Vergennes in 1814. For his "good conduct," he was promoted to lieutenant by Commodore Yeo. In contrast, the commander of the *Chub*, Lieutenant James McGhie, was as yet unproven. He would perform poorly in the battle, but his conduct had little influence on the outcome.

In contrast, all the American officers were young and untested. Macdonough had proven to be an energetic and resourceful young officer but had not yet risen to the rank of captain and had never commanded in battle. His junior officers were an uneven mix. On the *Saratoga*, he was without his highly regarded first lieutenant, Raymond Perry, due to sickness. Lieutenant Stephen Cassin on the *Ticonderoga* was a courageous officer who had already distinguished himself in the defense of Vergennes in May, but Lieutenant Charles Budd of the *Preble* would be found wanting in the coming battle. Budd had served with Macdonough before but lacked an exceptional record. Even though Macdonough characterized him as an "intemperate Man . . . careless or regardless of the service," still he selected Budd to command the sloop, a decision the U.S. commander would regret.[6]

Since arriving to take charge of the *Eagle*, Master Commandant Robert Henley had demonstrated an annoying lack of deference to Macdonough. Acting as if he had an independent command, he irritated the squadron commander by presuming that he, Henley, had the authority to name the *Eagle* and by communicating directly with

Secretary of the Navy Jones on several occasions rather than through the proper chain of command. Henley, who had just been promoted when he took command of the *Eagle* in August, was a headstrong officer with a checkered record. Macdonough thought him "to be very deficient in seamanship and in the equipment of a Vessel of War he is a stranger." Once ranking above Macdonough on the navy seniority list, Henley had been passed over for promotion on several occasions, having lost fifteen positions on the list between 1798 and 1815. He undoubtedly was miffed that his new commander had once been thirty positions beneath him. Henley also resented a negative performance evaluation that he had received from Lieutenant Cassin's father, Captain John Cassin, at the Norfolk Naval Yard. Macdonough later wrote that Henley's "disposition I take to be malicious."[7]

In a battle on the open waters of the lake, the long guns of the *Confiance* would probably have prevailed. Downie would likely have been able to maneuver his ship into a position beyond the effective range of the American carronades. Thus, while sustaining minimal damage, the *Confiance* could then have destroyed or battered the *Saratoga* into submission. Downie told Pring that he would "of course prefer fighting them [the Americans] on the Lake, and would wait until our Force is in an efficient state," but the captain mistakenly feared that Macdonough would "take shelter up the Lake, and not meet me on equals." But under pressure from Prevost to attack immediately, Downie did not have the opportunity or the time to try to lure his opponent onto the open waters and attack from long range. Instead, he decided to assault the American squadron where it lay anchored in the confined waters of Cumberland Bay.

An obvious question is why did Downie make this critical decision. Certainly, the British commander was under great pressure from Prevost to attack immediately, but he was rushing into battle with a flagship that was not completely finished and a crew that was not fully prepared. Although Downie never had the chance to explain himself later, he was apparently very confident, indeed overconfident, of victory. As an experienced and determined commander, he probably operated under the traditional expectation that the Royal Navy's "habit of victory" would produce success even under the most adverse circumstances. The decision to attack was also consistent with the aggressive British tactical doctrine of the time. As a combat veteran who had been commended for his previous conduct in action, Downie welcomed the chance to further distinguish himself by fighting rather than maneuvering. A product of Lord Nelson's navy, he embraced Nelson's famous dictum, "No captain can go far wrong if he places his ship alongside that of an enemy."[8]

Based on his own firsthand experience, Pring informed Downie that the U.S. "naval Force were well manned, and efficient in every respect." Disregarding this opinion, Downie responded that once British land forces had "stormed and taken possession of" the American shore batteries, the enemy squadron would be "obliged to quit their position whereby we shall obtain decided Advantage over them during their Confusion." He knew that he had superior officers and that Macdonough's undermanned and inexperienced crews were every bit as great a handicap as Downie's own crew. In fact, just two days before the battle, Prevost had informed him that "the American Fleet is insufficiently manned" and that the crew of the USS *Eagle* had been filled out at the last minute with "Prisoners of all descriptions" from the army. According to documents found later, "The strongest confidence prevailed in the superiority of the British vessels, their weight of metal, and in the capacity and experience of their officer[s] and crews; and as the commander of the forces was informed by an officer of the staff, who had been dispatched to Capt. Downie, that Capt. Downie credited himself with his own vessel alone a match for the whole American Squadron."[9]

After all, Downie was an experienced commander in the greatest navy in the world. Despite its unfinished condition, the *Confiance* was still a formidable ship with superior firepower. The frigate's gun crews were inexperienced by the standard of British blue-water fighting ships, but Downie had capable officers who knew their duties and how to execute them. The captain, then, was overconfident with very good reason. His counterpart was not even a first-line, senior American officer but a thirty-year-old master commandant of unknown and untested command ability.

After rounding Cumberland Head, the British ships planned to tack into the north-northeast wind, but the wind shifted to the west-northwest and then became a light and erratic breeze once they entered the bay. The baffling breeze prevented the British ships from reaching their intended positions. As a result, Downie was unable to fire a broadside at the *Eagle* but forced instead to head directly for the bow of the *Saratoga*. The Americans waited anxiously on their ships. Macdonough knelt on the deck of the *Saratoga* and led his men in prayer. Then he rose and ordered his signal midshipman to send a message: "Impressed seamen call upon every man to do his duty."[10] At about nine o'clock, the Americans fired the first shots when Henley prematurely discharged his guns from the *Eagle*. The shots fell well short of their intended target, the British flagship. Then as the *Linnet* sailed past the *Saratoga* to reach its position opposite the *Eagle*, the brig fired a broadside at Macdonough's ship. These shots also fell short, except for one that hit a chicken coop on the deck. A cock kept by the crew escaped, jumped on a gun slide, and crowed defiantly, according to eyewitnesses. Legend records that the *Saratoga*'s crew cheered the feisty bird as a good omen for the battle to come.[11]

The battle began in earnest when Macdonough sighted and fired a single gun from the *Saratoga* as the signal for his ships to begin their attack. Although the initial shots almost hit the *Confiance* and damaged two of its anchors in the port bow, Downie did not return fire until he had anchored his ship within four hundred yards of the *Saratoga*, well within the range of the Americans' carronades. The British commander patiently secured his decks, furled his sails, and sighted his port guns before firing a double-shotted broadside into the *Saratoga*'s hull. The devastating blast knocked half of its crew to the deck and killed or wounded forty men. Among the dead was 1st Lieutenant Peter Gamble.

The action was now fully underway. Rapid fire produced smoke and deafening noise. As a spectator near the tip of Cumberland Head, Julius Hubbell later remembered that "the firing was terrific, fairly shaking the ground, and so rapid that it seemed to be one continuous roar, intermingled with spiteful flashing from the mouths of the guns, and dense clouds of smoke soon hung over the two fleets."[12] About fifteen minutes after the fighting began, a shot from the *Saratoga* struck one of the guns on the *Confiance*, knocking it completely off its carriage and leveling Captain Downie. The blow killed the British commander instantly, even though his skin was not broken and the only visible sign of injury was a black streak across his chest. The impact had flattened his watch, its hands pointing to the exact moment of his death.[13]

Downie's death was a serious loss. Yet in the past, other British warships and squadrons had defeated their enemy after their senior commander had been killed or incapacitated in battle. Nearby in the *Linnet* was Captain Pring, a courageous and talented young officer who might have saved the day in similar fashion. But he never had the chance to take charge. First Lieutenant Robertson, now in command on the *Confiance*, was unable to send a messenger to Pring because the frigate's boats had been shot away. Then when Robertson tried to send a signal to the *Linnet*, he discovered that the ship's signal book had been lost in the confusion of combat. As a result, the British fleet was now without a commander.[14]

In the fierce fighting, the first ship to strike was the British sloop *Chub*. Fire from the *Eagle* had shot away its cables, bowsprit, sails, yards, and main boom. The *Chub* drifted helplessly between the battle line and then past the *Saratoga* while most of its officers and crew remained below deck. Its commander, Lieutenant McGhie, had two fingertips shot off and was wounded in the thigh by a splinter. Finally, with more than twenty casualties and only six men remaining on deck, McGhie gave the word from the *Chub*'s sickbay to surrender.

At the southern end of the line, a separate struggle was underway as HMS *Finch* and the British galleys attacked the *Preble* and the *Ticonderoga*. Since the *Finch* had difficulty sailing into position, it was unable to directly engage the *Ticonderoga*. Its commander, Lieutenant Hicks, later explained that his orders were only "to lead the Gun Boats in and support them" while engaging the *Preble*. As a result, *Finch* and *Preble* exchanged fire for nearly one hour before the American ship slipped anchor. According to the British, the *Preble* struck its colors as Lieutenant Budd moved his vessel close to the shoreline to escape the enemy guns. Although Budd denied this, British observers insisted that the *Preble* had lowered its colors and later rehoisted them.[15] In his postbattle report, Macdonough concluded that Budd "did not behave well on the 11th September."[16]

Meanwhile, British gunboats and USS *Ticonderoga* engaged in a fierce action. Three of the galleys each carried a 24-pound long gun, which had a greater range than any of the *Ticonderoga*'s guns, but the American ship's five carronades threatened any vessel that approached. Led by Lieutenant Mark Raynham in the *Yeo*, six gunboats moved to within three cables (a cable is 608 feet) of the American schooner. From there, Raynham gave the signal to approach but then abruptly pulled the *Yeo* out of the fight, reversed course, and headed for the tender HMS *Icicle*. Once there, the officer deserted his crew and leaped on board. When Raynham withdrew, Lieutenant James Bell in the gunboat HMS *Murray* had taken charge. When one of the other boats veered off in pursuit of the

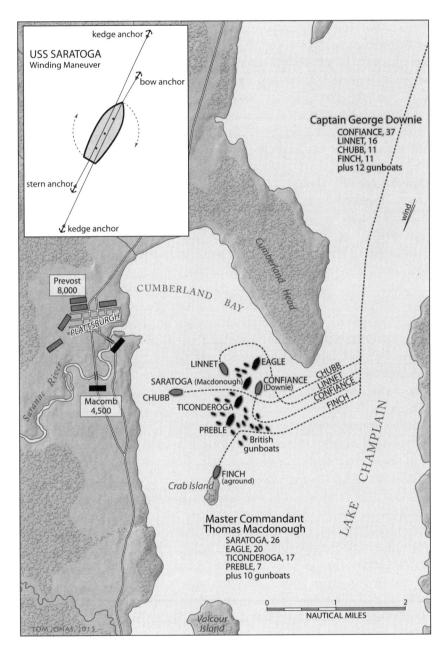

The Naval Battle of Lake Champlain and Macdonough's Winding Maneuver. Map by Tom Jonas, after original by William J. Clipson in Symonds, *Naval Institute Historical Atlas of the U.S. Navy*. Used by permission.

Preble, Bell led the remaining four in their attack. Under a barrage of British grape and musket shots, Cassin courageously directed the defense of his ship. As the enemy gunboats neared, Cassin expected support from the American gunboats assigned to assist him. Only one, the USS *Borer,* led by Midshipman Thomas Conover, tried to engage, but when it rounded the *Ticonderoga's* bow, a deadly volley struck the *Borer,* killing two men, wounding one other, and putting the gunboat out of the fight.[17] This brief diversion allowed Cassin to load his guns with canister and musket balls, depress the barrels, and fire a deadly blast. On Bell's own vessel, twenty-three men effectively deserted by lying down and refusing to fight. Nevertheless, the lieutenant valiantly led several more attempts that brought the gunboats close to the *Ticonderoga,* but Cassin's men repulsed all efforts. Bell himself was severely wounded, losing one leg above the knee, and was forced to leave the battle.[18]

After the gunboat attacks failed, HMS *Finch* engaged the *Ticonderoga* but was overmatched. Cassin fired a devastating broadside that severely damaged the *Finch's* main boom, mast, and rigging. After its rudder became inoperable, the British ship drifted off toward Crab Island and began to take on water. The sloop finally ran aground on a shoal extending from the island. There, convalescing soldiers at the hospital fired a gun at the grounded warship, which itself returned fire, forcing the Americans to take cover. Yet despite desperate efforts by Hicks to refloat his ship by pushing four carronades overboard and employing a kedge, the *Finch* remained grounded. Helplessly out of the battle, the lieutenant had no choice but to strike his colors.

Cassin's defense of the *Ticonderoga* made him one of the heroes of the day. In the fierce encounter, he had lost his first lieutenant, John Stansbury, to a cannonball that cut him in half, but the Americans' determination and courage prevailed. Macdonough later characterized Cassin as a "man of firmness when put to the test . . . whose Judgment is good, and who behaved very well on the 11th Sept. 1814." The *Ticonderoga* "gallantly sustained her full share of the Action," successfully fighting off both the British sloop and the gunboats. Had the schooner been boarded, the result of the naval battle might well have been different.[19]

Meanwhile, at the north end of the battle line, HMS *Confiance* and *Linnet* engaged in a fierce struggle with USS *Saratoga* and *Eagle.* After pounding the *Eagle,* the *Linnet's* guns shot away the starboard anchor spring of the *Eagle*, shifting it into a position that made its guns ineffective. Without orders from Macdonough nearby, Henley ordered the *Eagle's* cable cut. The American ship drifted and then reanchored between the *Saratoga* and the *Ticonderoga*, where it resumed the fight. But in removing his ship from the range of the *Linnet's* guns, that officer had now exposed the *Saratoga* to the "galling fire from the Enemy's brig [the *Linnet*]." In Macdonough's judgment, Henley had moved his ship prematurely. "I am decidedly of the opinion her duty was to remain in the station assigned her as long as it was possible for her to maintain it."[20]

As the deadly struggle continued, the noise, smoke, and chaos of battle reigned on both the American and British warships. Throughout the heat of combat, Macdonough assisted his gun crews like a common sailor. The American commander was injured and temporarily incapacitated twice. Shortly after the firing began, the severed piece of a spanker boom knocked Macdonough to the deck, where he lay unconscious for several minutes. He regained consciousness and returned to action, but later he was hit in the face by the flying head of a gun captain, decapitated by a British cannonball. Stunned, Macdonough again returned to the fight after a few moments.[21]

In the chaos of battle, Macdonough and Robertson managed to maintain order and continue firing from their respective flagships. Inevitably, however, some of their guns suffered damage, and their crews made mistakes that reduced the number and effectiveness of others. On the *Saratoga* the Americans overloaded some of their carronades with shot as far as the muzzle. On the *Confiance* the inexperienced gun crews made similar mistakes. One crew loaded a cannon with two balls but no powder, another with powder but no shot, and a third with the cartridge and the wad in reverse order. Such errors from inexperienced crews in the heat of battle were predictable but did not prevent either side from continuing to fire. But the recently formed crews of the *Confiance* repeatedly made the same costly mistake, failing to push the quoin, or gun wedge, back under the rear of the carriage after firing each shot. Typically, the backlash of the carriage loosened or dislodged the quoin when the gun was fired. Since both the *Confiance* and the *Saratoga* were anchored at close range under calm conditions, there probably seemed no reason to force the quoin back into place after the guns had been sighted initially. But as the quoins worked loose from under the carriages, the direction of the muzzles was gradually elevated. As a result, Macdonough later reported, many of the "enemy's shot passed principally just over our [the Americans'] heads."[22] Nevertheless, severe damage still resulted as the yards, masts, rigging, and hammocks were struck and crashed to the deck. The hull of the *Saratoga*, though, received many fewer direct hits and less damage than did the hull of the *Confiance*.

After nearly two hours of combat from anchored positions, the frequency and intensity of fire gradually diminished as the guns on both flagships were disabled. Only four port guns on the *Confiance* remained in service, while the *Saratoga*'s starboard guns were "nearly all dismounted, or not manageable."[23] Once the *Eagle* had left her position, the *Linnet* drove off several American gunboats and concentrated her guns on the *Saratoga*. With a fire burning on deck and the last of its starboard carronades disabled, the *Saratoga* was in a desperate situation.

At this crucial moment Macdonough made the decision that saved the day by giving the order to wind, or turn, his ship. The *Saratoga*'s crew disengaged the stern anchor and cut the bow cable. As the ship turned slowly, one of its lines stuck, but under great duress the crew struggled and managed to free it, thus allowing the *Saratoga* to be turned from end to end. Macdonough's planning, preparation, and leadership proved critical now. Under fire in the chaos of combat, the commander maintained self-control, and his well-disciplined men followed orders. With his ship winded, Macdonough now brought his fresh and undamaged port guns to bear on the *Confiance*. Since his port guns had also been disabled, Lieutenant Robertson attempted to duplicate this maneuver, but in the middle of the attempt, as the frigate's starboard broadside "near got to bear on the Enemy again," the cable stuck and tangled, thus leaving the *Confiance* in a vulnerable position, with its bow facing the *Saratoga*. Without the presence of Captain Downie, inexperience and lack of training took a critical toll. The "Ship's Company declared they would stand no longer to their Quarters, nor could the Officers with their utmost exertions rally them."[24]

It was now the *Confiance* that was in a desperate state. Damage to the ship was extensive. Its hull shattered, the frigate could not be maneuvered. Dead and wounded crewmen littered the bloody decks. To make room, some of the dead were thrown overboard while many of the wounded had to be "frequently moved from place to place to prevent their being drowned" below deck. Robertson made a final attempt to save the ship by signaling British gunboats to come to his assistance, but the effort failed. He then convened his surviving officers, and together they decided to strike the colors since any further resistance would "be a Wanton and useless waste of human blood."[25]

Once the *Confiance* struck, the *Saratoga* shifted its guns to the *Linnet*. With its sails, riggings, and masts destroyed, the brig was unable to flee and thereby forced to surrender. The *Linnet* had more than a foot of water on its lower deck, and there was no chance of being rescued by the British galleys, which had fled the battle scene. Once the *Linnet* surrendered, Macdonough ordered the remaining American gunboats to chase the withdrawing galleys but then rescinded the order so that the American boats could assist and help save the heavily damaged larger ships. As the enemy gunboats fled north, American spectators on Cumberland Head celebrated by cheering, banging pans, ringing bells, and blowing horns. The passing British ships silenced the joyous racket with a single cannon shot.

The battle had lasted about two and one-half hours. Although most of the British and American galleys and gunboats had survived, the four large British ships had been destroyed or disabled, while damage to the four large American ships had been extensive. At the end of the fighting, none of the large ships on either side was capable of sailing on its own. Shortly afterward, the twenty-six-year-old Hubbell, who had witnessed the fighting from atop Cumberland Head, visited both flagships. On the *Saratoga* he spoke with Macdonough and noted that although the decks had been cleaned and the dead and been packed up in order, the ship's seams were still "full of blood, and the torn hull, masts and spars told the story of the fearful struggle." The condition of the *Confiance* presented "a horrible sight." There Hubbell found the vessel to be "absolutely torn to pieces, the decks were strewed with mutilated bodies lying in all directions, and everything was covered with blood. It was the most fearful sight I ever beheld." Midshipman Robert Lea explained, "all our masts, yards and sails [were] so shattered that one looked like so many bunches of matches, the other like a bundle of old rags."[26]

Damage to the warships demonstrated that the fighting had been fierce. The hull of the *Confiance* had taken 105 hits; the *Saratoga* had absorbed 55 to its hull. The *Linnet* took an estimated 50 total hits and the *Eagle* 39. Although the British disputed and denied his claim, Macdonough reported that his flagship had twice been set on fire by hotshot from the *Confiance*.[27] In addition to the typical devastation of masts and spars crashing to the decks, an inordinate number of splinters from the deck and hulls of the ships flew around, missiles made more deadly by the use of soft, green, and readily available pine and oak rather than the heavy seasoned oak used to build most oceangoing warships. "The havoc on both sides was dreadful," observed Midshipman Lea. "Never was a shower of hail so thick as the shot whistling about our ears. . . . [M]y jacket, waistcoat, trouser and hat . . . are literally torn all to rags with shot and splinters." Lea also reported that "one of the marines who was in the Trafalgar action with Lord Nelson, says it was a mere fleabite in comparison to this."[28]

Reflecting the devastation to the ships was the considerable damage to men. Macdonough reported fifty-two dead and fifty-eight wounded, but of the latter he apparently counted only those who entered the hospital; ninety other Americans were less seriously wounded. The British suffered an estimated fifty-eight dead and 116 wounded. The *Confiance* experienced the heaviest casualties. The British having thrown some of their dead overboard in the heat of battle, bodies floated in the bay for days afterward.[29]

The naval battle of Lake Champlain had been a tense, brutal, and closely fought affair, with critical moments and developments that might have decided the result in the favor of either squadron. But in the end, the outcome was determined by a combination of careful planning and execution, great courage and brilliant leadership, and by both luck (or the lack thereof) and human mistakes or failures.

The Americans were better prepared and had planned more carefully than the British. An important factor in the prebattle preparation was the level of cooperation on each side. Macdonough and Macomb had their differences, but they worked well together. They agreed upon their objective and the deployment of their respective forces to achieve it. Most important were the soldiers who Macomb agreed to send to help fill out the undermanned crews. Needing these men for his greatly outnumbered army on shore, it would have been easy for the general to deny Macdonough's request, but he chose not to. In a war that more often witnessed discord and bickering between American military commanders, Macdonough and Macomb's cooperation is exemplary.

In sharp contrast, the British command was in some disarray. Prevost did not have the full support he needed from Yeo to complete construction and fully man the *Confiance* in a timely manner. He also had to contend with an abrupt command change when Downie took charge on September 1. Henceforth, the two commanders' relations were professional but cold and even sarcastic on the eve of the battle. Prevost resented having to wait until the eleventh to attack American forces in Plattsburgh. Meanwhile, Downie sought several more days to prepare properly. Then, without a well-coordinated battle plan, the simultaneous naval and land assault that the captain believed he had been promised by Prevost never materialized on September 11. Shortly after British troops belatedly forded the Saranac River, the British warships struck their colors in the bay.

For the Americans, Macdonough's preparation and execution proved decisive. He had carefully anchored his ships in a position that forced the enemy to fight on his terms in a confined space. Under pressure to attack and with assurances that Prevost would simultaneously assault enemy positions on shore, Downie willingly entered the Americans' selected battle area. In choosing to engage them at relatively close range, Downie reduced the advantage that his superior long guns gave him and increased the destructive power of Macdonough's carronades. Both naval commanders secured their respective ships at anchor so that they might be turned, or winded, in battle to bring a set of broadside guns into action. When all of his port guns were put out of action, Macdonough chose that precise moment to wind his ship. The discipline of his crew under his strong leadership ensured that the maneuver was successfully executed under fire. Once Robertson on the *Confiance* was unable to duplicate Macdonough's maneuver, the outcome was determined.

Generally, both sides fought well and courageously, but a combination of luck and mistakes shaped the outcome. Downie's death early in the battle was a critical event, particularly since its effect was magnified by the inability of Lieutenant Robertson to communicate with the squadron's second in command, Captain Pring on HMS *Linnet*. Either fate or misfortunate determined that when he needed them, Robertson's boats had been shot away and the *Confiance*'s signal book had disappeared. Similarly, the fact that Macdonough was twice knocked unconscious but rose to continue the fight was crucial for the Americans.

Although crewmen on both sides made mistakes, the inexperience of the *Confiance*'s gun crews proved more important. By failing
to reset the quoins, or gun wedges, after they fired each round, the
men unknowingly raised the elevation of their guns, thus significantly reducing damage to USS *Saratoga*. As a result, the more heavily armed *Confiance* lost an important part of its advantage over the
smaller American flagship.

Certainly, there were individual heroics and failures on both
sides. For the Americans, Lieutenant Cassin's courage and leadership saved USS *Ticonderoga*, whereas Master Commandant Henley
and Lieutenant Budd did not perform well. For the British, Robertson
and Pring fought bravely and tenaciously, while Lieutenants McGhie
and Raynham performed poorly and later deserted. On HMS *Finch*
Lieutenant Hicks's performance was questionable. While he forced
USS *Preble* to flee, Hicks clearly did not engage the *Ticonderoga*
directly as he had been ordered to do. Then he grounded his ship on
a shoal extending from Crab Island. At the naval court-martial in
1815, Hicks blamed his pilot. Other testimony indicated that the
British had only one chart of the lake, which was in the possession
of Pring and apparently had not been available to Hicks.

On shore the British attack did not begin until the naval battle
was well underway. Prevost planned for Major General Brisbane's
brigade, supported by guns from the British batteries in Plattsburgh,
to attack the two bridges across the Saranac River. Meanwhile, a
much larger force commanded by Major General Robinson and supported by regiments from Major General Power's brigade would
ford the river three miles to the west, where it was shallow and
the American positions were weak. Once across, Robinson's force
would then turn and assault General Macomb's principal posts in
Plattsburgh from the flank and the rear.[30]

Across the river at Pike's Ford, several hundred American militiamen were hidden and waited along the road south toward the
settlement on the Salmon River. Since most of these troops were
green and poorly armed volunteers, Macomb did not expect them to
make a stand between the crossing and Plattsburgh. Instead, he had
ordered them to fall back along the road and thus draw the British
south rather than have the enemy turn east back toward the
American works in Plattsburgh.[31]

Prevost's plan was poorly executed. Although Downie insisted
that Prevost had promised to attack promptly when the naval

battle began, the land assault lagged. In Plattsburgh the army shelled American fortifications but did not try to cross the main bridges and overrun these positions. Meanwhile, the advance to the west went slowly. Although Robinson had his force ready before dawn, he did not receive his final orders from Prevost until after eight o'clock. The British began their march before ten o'clock. With no main road along the river, where trees and vegetation were dense, the British had not scouted and identified the best route upstream. Officers later complained that Prevost had not prepared a precise battle plan and in Plattsburgh had refused to pay to acquire accurate local intelligence. As a result, the British lost one hour while having to retrace their steps to find the correct route. It was not until after eleven o'clock that Robinson's force finally reached Pike's Ford. Across the river, with no field artillery, Vermont major general Samuel Strong had divided his militiamen and moved them from the riverbank to the edge of the nearby forest.[32] Had they crossed and sent the Americans scurrying one hour before they did, the British might well have over-whelmed and occupied Macomb's forts in Plattsburgh by the time that the naval fight ended. Given Prevost's defensive mindset, he might still have decided on a strategic retreat but could have claimed a victory over American land forces in justifying his withdrawal.

When finally in position, General Robinson sent Power's brigade across the river first. Supported by a 6-pound field gun, the British crossed easily, dislodged the Americans, and sent most of them scurrying toward the settlement of Salmon. Having followed Power across the Saranac, Robinson then turned his forces ninety degrees to the left, or east, and began to head for Plattsburgh. Without sig-nificant resistance, the British moved quickly. As the inexperienced militiamen fled south, an easy victory seemed at hand.

It was at that moment in the early afternoon that an aide from Prevost caught up with Robinson and delivered the message that the naval battle had been lost and he was to retreat immediately. In Plattsburgh Prevost had followed the engagement closely and was mortified to hear shouts of an American victory ring across the bay. In an order issued at noon, he decided to end his offensive, aban-don his foothold in the town, and withdraw all of his ground forces immediately. Prevost later explained that the unexpected American victory deprived him "of the cooperation of the Fleet without which the further prosecution of the service was become impracti-cal." He also apparently believed that a large number of American reinforcements were on their way. In this situation Prevost no doubt remembered that his official orders had emphasized, "Always . . . taking care not [to] expose His Majesty's Forces to being cut off by too extended a line of advance."[33]

The order to withdraw stunned Robinson and his fellow officers. With victory seemingly in their grasp, Prevost inexplicably had called a halt. The general later wrote of the effect when word spread: "Never was [there] anything like the disappointment expressed in every countenance. The advance was within shot, and full view of the Redoubt, and in one hour they must have been ours. We retired . . . in as much silent discontent as was ever exhibited." One of his advance units did not get the initial orders, and when the main column began to retreat, most in that detached company were killed or taken prisoner by General Strong's militia.[34]

The retreating generals were a frustrated and angry lot, agreeing that there was no justification for Prevost's abrupt decision. These toughened veterans of Wellington's European campaigns believed that Plattsburgh could have been taken and held with little trouble. Moreover, once in control of the town and its batteries, there would be little threat from U.S. naval forces—after all, the small squadron must have been seriously damaged in its victory. Nothing they learned later would change their opinion of the operation. Although Prevost did not realize it at the time, his conduct in Plattsburgh had created two intractable enemies. In the weeks and months ahead, both British navy and army officials would place the embarrassing defeat squarely on the governor in chief.

Although most historians defend Prevost's decision to withdraw, it was very controversial at the time. He himself explained that the "disastrous and unlooked for result of the Naval Contest" deprived him of the "only means by which I could avail myself of any advantage I might gain," rendering continuation of the attack "highly imprudent, as well as hazardous." Since "the Enemy's Militia was rising En Masse around me," Provost feared being cut off by bad weather and obstructed roads. Under the circumstances, he had to decide "whether I should consider my own Fame by gratifying the Ardor of the Troops . . . or consult the more substantial interests of my Country by withdrawing the Army which was yet uncrippled for the security of these Provinces." Had he persevered and failed in his attack, "the destruction of a great part of my Troops must have been the consequence, and with the remainder I should have had to make a precipitate and embarrassed retreat, one very different from that which I have made."[35]

The retreat began almost immediately. To cover the withdrawal, British artillery continued to fire until late afternoon on September 11, and then at 9:00 P.M. Prevost began to withdraw his guns and some of his baggage. At 2:00 A.M. the next morning, "the whole Army precipitately retreated, leaving the sick and wounded to our generousity," reported Macomb. Although rains and bad roads slowed their twenty-five-mile march, British forces began recrossing into Canada on September 14, completing their withdrawal from American territory by September 25. Army loses were light: forty-seven killed, 221 wounded, seventy taken prisoner, and 234 deserted. In their wake the British left large amounts of supplies, provisions, and arms. Near Isle La Motte, a supply ship carrying a large amount of ordnance sank and was later recovered by the Americans.[36]

Shortly after the naval battle ended, Macdonough wrote a brief note to Secretary of the Navy Jones amid the exhaustion, suffering, and devastation around him. "The Almighty has been pleased to grant us a signal victory on Lake Champlain in the capture of one frigate, one brig, and two sloops of war of the enemy."[37] Soon, the four surviving commanders of the British squadron came aboard the *Saratoga* to present their swords to Macdonough. When Captain Pring and Lieutenants Robertson, McGhie, and Hicks made their symbolic gesture, the American commander magnanimously refused to receive them: "Gentlemen, return your swords to your scabbards and wear them. You are worthy of them."[38] On Crab Island the hospital treated the wounded from both sides. Macdonough paroled forty-seven of the most seriously injured British and sent them to Isle-aux-Noix. The British and American dead were buried side by side on Crab Island in unmarked graves. The bodies of the dead officers, including Captain Downie, were covered with flags and interred in a formal ceremony three days later. Macdonough sent 367 enemy prisoners south on the steamer *Vermont*.[39]

In appreciation for their generous treatment, the officers of HMS *Linnet* and HMS *Confiance* thanked Macdonough. Speaking for his officers, Robertson praised him for the "unbounded liberality and humane treatment not only extended to themselves [the officers] but to the unfortunate wounded seamen and marines."[40]

The battle on the lake and on the land was over, resulting in a decisive American naval victory that Prevost believed gave him no reasonable alternative but to withdraw immediately. In Plattsburgh as the American soldiers dispersed, they left buildings and dwellings that had been destroyed or badly burned. The militia disappeared quickly, including Aikin's Rifle Company, which disbanded on September 12. Although normal peacetime routines would not return locally for weeks, combat operations had ceased. But the repercussions of this brief and critical struggle would soon be felt and continue to ripple out for months in Canada and Washington, D.C., as well as far away in London and Ghent.

CHAPTER 5

REPERCUSSIONS

CANADA AND THE UNITED STATES

The Battle of Lake Champlain (and Plattsburgh) had far-reaching repercussions that surfaced unevenly during the fall of 1814 due to the considerable amount of time that it took for news to travel in the early nineteenth century. Steam power existed, but it did not yet propel railroad locomotives, and small steamships could travel only short distances. Telegraph communication was still decades away. Information and news still traveled only as fast as messengers on horses, carriages pulled by horses, or sail-powered ships could carry them. For example, word of the momentous American victory on Lake Champlain and the precipitous British withdrawal from Plattsburgh on September 11 did not reach London for more than one month and the negotiators at Ghent for five weeks. In North America the news reached Montreal, Quebec, and nearby towns in New England quickly, but it took days to reach Boston, New York, and Philadelphia. And this dramatic event was not generally known in Washington, D.C., until newspapers published it on Monday, September 19, eight days after the battle.

On the scene in Plattsburgh, the results of the battle were evident, but the immediate future was unclear. The British retreat across the border into Canada was well known, for they had left behind their wounded, hundreds of deserters, and a huge amount of supplies and ordnance, including the supply ship that had sunk near Isle La Motte (which Macdonough's men later recovered). The British presence on Lake Champlain had ceased to exist. The tender HMS *Icicle* and the British gunboats had scurried back to the Richelieu River. The severely damaged *Confiance*, *Linnet*, *Finch*, and *Chub* had survived but were in American hands. Two of their surviving officers, Lieutenant McGhie, commander of the *Chub*, and Lieutenant Raynham, the leader of the gunboat assault, deserted rather than face questions about their conduct in the battle. Meanwhile, the largest U.S. ships had survived but also had suffered serious damage. The destruction to the decks, masts, spars, and sails rendered all of these largest warships temporarily inoperable. One of Macdonough's first tasks, therefore, was to repair these vessels. On October 2 he sent the *Saratoga, Ticonderoga, Confiance,* and *Linnet* to Whitehall at the south end of the lake. He kept the *Eagle, Preble, Montgomery,* and ten gunboats at Plattsburgh to perform various tasks. Also stationed there were the *Finch* and the *Chub,* which had been restored and renamed USS *Growler* and USS *Eagle.*[1]

Both Macdonough and Macomb expected the British army to attack again either in the fall or winter. Although the enemy squadron had been captured and could not be replaced for months, the huge and formidable invading army lurked nearby across the border. Would it remain there? One telling indicator that it might not was the level of smuggling activity from Vermont across the border, which much to the chagrin of Customs Agent Peter Sailly, remained high through October and November 1814. American units on both sides of the lake remained on alert, and Macomb began to build two new forts to protect the southern routes into Plattsburgh. Although they proved mistaken, both American commanders believed that the British had not intended originally to halt their invasion at Plattsburgh but to continue to the south end of the lake and possibly beyond to the Hudson River. Macdonough and his officers believed that the British would invade again in an effort to either capture or destroy the naval squadron while in winter quarters. Accordingly, he intended to keep his fleet at Whitehall for the winter, sending his remaining ships south from Plattsburgh in November.[2]

In fact, rumors spread that a winter campaign was imminent. There were reports of men and equipment, including 1,000 sleighs and 10,000 buffalo robes, being sent to Isle-aux-Noix for a winter offensive. Prevost actually considered a proposal to attack the American fleet at Whitehall during the winter, but he rejected the idea because of the harsh conditions and distances involved as well as the likelihood of further desertions from his army during such an expedition.[3]

As Macdonough and Macomb went about various postbattle routines and prepared for an anticipated second British offensive, the two men were showered with public praise and commendations. The citizens of Plattsburgh gave a formal dinner in Macdonough's honor on September 23. Provided with food, spirits, and cigars, those present drank eighteen formal toasts accompanied by cannon fire and music from Macomb's army band. When it was his turn, in typically modest fashion, Macdonough merely toasted the "memory of Commodore Downie, our brave enemy," while Macomb saluted the New York and Vermont volunteers: "Our friends in need; our friends indeed." Three days later on the twenty-sixth, the citizens of Burlington hosted another dinner in which the crowd saluted the victors with twenty-one toasts. Macdonough was also honored with substantial gifts. The state of New York gave him one thousand acres of land in Cayuga County; Vermont presented him with one hundred acres on Cumberland Head. His home state of Delaware presented him with a sword and a complete silver service. The city of Albany gave him "its freedom" and a plot of land in Washington Square.[4]

New York City had portraits of both Macdonough and Macomb painted and hung in city hall. Congress acknowledged both men in resolutions of thanks, struck a gold medal for each, and promoted each officer effective the day of the battle, Macdonough to captain and Macomb to major general. Both heroes received numerous other honors and gifts as the weeks passed.[5] Speaking in support of a congressional resolution on the "importance and brilliancy" of Macdonough's triumph, Representative James Pleasants of Virginia labeled the victory equal to any ever achieved by the navy and "in its consequences certainly surpassed by none." "The Americans were, in every sense of the word, fighting for their country" because Governor in Chief Prevost was determined "to lay waste and destroy all the assailable parts of our country." As a victorious naval commander, Macdonough was also entitled to prize money for his capture of the British warships. The total amount came to $329,000; Macdonough's share was $22,807.[6]

Although the Navy Department did not release the captain from his command, it granted him leave to spend several weeks with his family in Middletown in December. There he saw his six-week-old son for the first time. By early January 1815, Macdonough was back on Lake Champlain, where he and Macomb would remain until the news of a peace treaty arrived in February.

In the immediate aftermath of victory, Macdonough selected Lieutenant Cassin for the honor of conveying his victory dispatches and the flags of the surrendered enemy ships to Secretary of the Navy Jones in Washington. As commander of the *Ticonderoga* during the battle, Cassin had been instrumental, Macdonough praising him as a man of "firmness when put to the test . . . who behaved very well on the 11th Sept. 1814." After leaving on September 13, Cassin was briefly welcomed by Major DeWitt Clinton in New York City, where he learned of the successful defense of Baltimore. Arriving in that city, the victorious defenders of Fort McHenry honored the Plattsburgh and Lake Champlain victories at noon on Sunday the eighteenth with a "federal salute," consisting of repeated volleys from the fort's guns.[7]

The governors of both New York and Vermont capitalized politically on the victory. In New York, Governor Daniel Tompkins was a Republican supporter of the Madison administration in a state where another Republican faction, the followers of Major Clinton, hoped to unseat the president in 1816. A committed and resourceful prowar governor, Tompkins had done all that he could to support the extensive military activities along his state's borders, including spending funds not authorized by the legislature. In a speech to state lawmakers after the victory, Tompkins underlined the extent of the threat posed by Prevost's invasion, claiming that the "one great object . . . was to penetrate . . . Lake Champlain and the Hudson, and, by a simultaneous attack with his maritime force on New York [City], to form a junction which should sever the communications of the States." In recognition of Tompkins's service and talent, Madison asked him to become secretary of state in the fall of 1814. The governor declined, however, because he believed it necessary to remain in New York to defend himself against political attacks on his unauthorized wartime expenditures.[8]

In sharp contrast to Tompkins, Governor Chittenden of Vermont had been a strong antiwar Federalist. When the popular election did not produce a clear gubernatorial victory in 1813, the Vermont assembly selected Chittenden as governor in a close vote. An outspoken opponent of the war and the Madison administration, Chittenden had recalled the Vermont militia from serving in New York during the fall of 1813. His action created outrage as the militia officers refused to leave that state, and some congressmen started an unsuccessful effort to have Chittenden prosecuted in federal court. Although he opposed the war as "unnecessary, unwise and hopeless in its offensive operations," Chittenden vigorously defended Vermont. In the spring of 1814, he sent the militia to fortify and defend Burlington and Vergennes from a British attack, efforts that helped save Macdonough's ships at Otter Creek. Then in late

August 1814, as the invasion from Canada loomed, the governor refused to send the Vermont militia to Plattsburgh, instead calling for volunteers. Under the command of Major General Strong, an estimated 2,500 men volunteered to defend Plattsburgh, although most of them arrived too late to fight in the battle.[9]

After the battle Chittenden publicly praised Macdonough and Macomb while extolling their victory. In October, when the Vermont legislature reconvened, the governor lauded the Americans at Plattsburgh for teaching the invaders "the mortifying lesson, that the soil of freedom will not bear the tread of hostile feet with impunity." In a moment of political hyperbole, he declared that the victory had "not [been] surpassed in the records of naval and military warfare." The American triumph had not, however, converted Chittenden into a supporter of the war or of the president. He supported the calling of the Hartford Convention. When the Vermont legislature declined the invitation by Massachusetts to send delegates, Chittenden sent his secretary of state as an unofficial observer.[10] That fall he was again narrowly reelected governor.

In Washington the news during early September had been consistently bad. On the ninth the *National Intelligencer* announced that Castine, Maine, and Prairie du Chien had fallen and that Philadelphia banks had suspended specie payments.[11] Four days later the paper reported that the British had been sighted at Baltimore and that the frigate USS *Adams* had been lost in Maine. Another item noted that Plattsburgh was about to fall. Finally came some unexpected positive news. First was a report that the Americans had repulsed the British at nearby Baltimore, then that the Americans had turned back an invasion at Lake Champlain. "GLORIOUS NEWS," proclaimed the *National Intelligencer* when it received the news of the "annihilation of the British Naval force on Lake Champlain and the defeat of the very large British army at the head of the lake." The paper noted that the "recent victory has everywhere diffused heartfelt joy, and been received with welcome salutations."[12]

The timing of this news from Lake Champlain was important because Congress was to convene on September 19. President Madison and his beleaguered administration sorely needed positive developments in the war.[13] Although the British had been turned back on Lake Champlain and at Baltimore, no one yet knew where the enemy's Chesapeake armada or the invasion force in Canada would head next. Rumors were plentiful. Some thought Philadelphia or New York City would be next targets; others expected an invasion of Rhode Island. Many in Massachusetts expected an attack on Boston. Farther north, another offensive on either Lake Champlain or against Sackets Harbor seemed likely.

In fact, the administration and the nation faced a genuine crisis. Secretary of the Navy Jones called the nation's affairs "as gloomy as can well be." From New York the *National Advocate* declared, "These may be truly said to be *the times that try men's souls.*" "I am impressed with the importance of the present crisis," wrote a Republican congressman from Massachusetts, "and the importance of the adoption of strong and energetic measures."[14]

In the smoldering aftermath of the attack on Washington, Madison had restored a semblance of order by returning quickly to the capital and resuming governmental activities. His September 1 proclamation had reassured the American people that their government was operating and that the defense of the country was intact.[15] But Madison's cabinet was in disarray, with critical vacancies in the War, Treasury, and Navy Departments. Secretary of War Armstrong was gone, Treasury Secretary Gerald Campbell resigned in September, and Secretary Jones had informed the president that he would leave his position no later than December 1 because of personal financial difficulties. In the interim Secretary of State Monroe oversaw the War Department as well, but Madison still needed to find long-term replacements for these positions.

More serious than the president's immediate cabinet problems were the nation's manpower and financial crises. If the war was to be continued, the administration needed many more troops and the money to pay for them. Monroe estimated that given the current effective regular and volunteer forces of only 30,000 men, the United States would need to raise an additional 30,000 regulars and 40,000 volunteers to wage the war properly. By September 1814, the government essentially had run out of funds too, with scant hopes of raising money. The charter of the Bank of the United States, which had been allowed to expire in 1811, had not been replaced. A number of state banks in the Mid-Atlantic region and in New England had suspended specie payments and were unable to loan the federal government money. In addition, large tax increases seemed politically out of the question.

The city itself also presented a depressing sight. Public buildings lay in charred ruins. Congress was scheduled to convene on

September 19, but the Capitol had been destroyed. The only possible place for the legislators to meet was the Patent Office, which had been spared, but quarters there would be cramped and difficult. The government brought in carpenters to renovate the building's interior, but when the work was finished, there were still not enough seats. Department heads did their best to rent private buildings from which to conduct their administrative business. "The ruins of the public edifices," said Jonathan Roberts, "is more complete than I had anticipated." With the exception of the French, European diplomats moved to Philadelphia. Moreover, accommodations were more scarce and crowded than usual. "I am surrounded," wrote William Wirt, "by a vast crowd & bustle of legislators and gentlemen of the turf assembled for the [horse] races which commence here tomorrow."[16]

In his September 20 message to Congress, the president castigated the enemy, reviewed recent American military successes, and asked for the resources required to win a nasty war against a formidable and arrogant foe. Madison condemned the British for "trampling on the usages of civilized warfare, and . . . in the plunder and wanton destruction of private property." This "barbarous policy has not even spared those monuments of the arts and models of taste" in the nation's capital.[17] In reviewing recent military events, Madison argued that U.S. successes far outweighed its military defeats in 1814. He cited the exploits of Captain David Porter in the Pacific, successful naval cruises, and the ongoing effectiveness of American privateers. He also praised the splendid victories on the Niagara frontier, in the South against hostile Indians, in the defense of Baltimore, and on Lake Champlain. With respect to the latter, Madison placed the victory into the broader military picture but lauded Macdonough in particular. "The best praise for this officer and his intrepid comrades is in the likeness of his triumph to the illustrious victory which immortalized another officer [Oliver Hazard Perry]" who won command of Lake Erie. The president predicted that despite the best efforts of the enemy, the American people would again prevail just as they had in "their revolutionary struggle" of the previous century.[18]

To Madison, the military lesson of 1814 was clear. American successes foretold eventual victory, but the end of the war was not at hand. The conflict would have to be continued for the foreseeable future. To do that, the president asked Congress to fill the ranks of the regular army, increase the number of volunteers, and furnish "large sums" of money to fund the war effort. "It is not to be disguised that the situation of our country calls for its greatest efforts. Our enemy is powerful in men and in money, on the land and on the water. Availing himself of fortuitous advantages, he is aiming with his undivided force a deadly blow at our growing prosperity, perhaps at our national existence." He predicted that the people would "cheerfully and proudly bear every burden of every kind which the safety and honor of the nation demand."[19]

Madison's call for the nation to sacrifice to see the war through fell on a group of sullen and fractious lawmakers. "Congress have met in a bad temper, grumbling at everything in order to avert the responsibility which they have incurred in refusing to provide the solid foundations for revenue and relying upon loans," reported Secretary Jones. "They have suffered the specie to go out of the country, adopted a half-way system of taxation, refused or omitted to establish in due time a national bank, and yet expect the war to be carried on with energy." Although the Republicans maintained large majorities in both the House and the Senate, their margins were misleading because they were divided among themselves. A significant minority within their ranks continued to be critical of Madison and opposed to his administration's legislative agenda.[20]

The news from Lake Champlain and Baltimore helped restore confidence in the administration it also removed pressure on Congress to act quickly and decisively. Suddenly, the crisis did not seem so dire. Baltimore had been saved, and the British had retreated from New York into Canada. In response, Congress acted in a typically dilatory manner in the fall of 1814. Rather than focusing on war measures, it spent the first several weeks of the session debating the distracting question of whether the nation's capital should remain in Washington or be relocated to another site. For those northerners who did not like the climate and inconveniences of Washington, the burning of the town presented an opportunity to move the federal seat north to its previous site at Philadelphia. It was not until November that Congress made the decision—on sectional votes and by small margins—not to relocate.

During these weeks, Madison managed to keep his administration functioning by patching the holes in his cabinet. First, he allowed Monroe to become secretary of war while continuing to serve as secretary of state. Secretary of the Navy Jones insisted on resigning, though he did not do so until December. Finally, for the critical position of secretary of the Treasury, Madison selected Alexander Dallas from Pennsylvania. Born in Jamaica and educated in England, Dallas was a capable man with an excellent understanding of public finance, but he was also a very unpopular individual in his home state.

Congress moved slowly but eventually addressed the need for additional troops and money to wage the war. As a result, the September crisis of 1814 had passed by the time the congressmen dealt with most of the issues before them. Monroe wanted 30,000 more regular-army soldiers and 40,000 additional volunteers. To ensure that these numbers were achieved, he also pressed for a conscription system. Eventually, Congress authorized 40,000 volunteers and allowed up to 40,000 state-militia troops being called into federal service, but it refused to institute conscription. On financial issues legislators also balked. To fund the war, Treasury Secretary Dallas wanted to issue treasury notes, levy new taxes, and reestablish a national bank. In October Congress authorized the issuance of $10.5 million in notes and $3 million in additional loans. Later in the session lawmakers approved extensive new taxes but defeated the bill to create a new national bank.[21]

By October, military events had been instrumental in diffusing the political crisis in New England. First came the news from Lake Champlain and Baltimore, then word arrived that the British had disappeared altogether from Chesapeake Bay. There were no reports of an attack on New York or Philadelphia. In Boston days and then weeks passed without an enemy assault on the city materializing. Still, opposition to the war and criticism of the federal government remained strong because the coastline remained undefended and peace did not seem imminent. Nevertheless, when the special session of the Massachusetts legislature met in early October, the political environment had moderated considerably. The General Court quickly adopted a report that called for a convention of New England states to recommend measures to address their grievances against the federal government. But the convention movement was controlled by moderate Federalists such as Harrison Gray Otis, not by that party's extremists. First Connecticut and then Rhode Island followed the lead of Massachusetts, but New Hampshire and Vermont decided not to participate, although delegates from each state attended. The convention would convene in December in

Hartford, Connecticut, but it was clear weeks before it met that the Hartford Convention would not be a meeting of dangerous or secessionist extremists.[22]

The situation in Canada was very different. Although the British invasion had failed, Montreal and all of Lower Canada remained secure. In fact, the Americans were in no position to pursue further victories. Their navy was temporarily physically incapable of conducting operations, and Macomb's defense force was considerably smaller than the British army that stood between it and Montreal. But the defeat created a firestorm of criticism and controversy in Canada which soon spread to London. Some of the postbattle controversy involved standard interservice rivalry and backbiting as officers blamed each other for not doing their jobs. But very soon criticism from both army and navy officers focused on the person and the conduct of Governor in Chief Sir George Prevost.

Prevost seems not to have realized initially the intensity of the criticism that he would incur, but his eighteen-year-old daughter, Ann, was immediately concerned about the effect that the retreat from Plattsburgh would have on her father's reputation. Mortified when she learned of the defeat, Ann confided to her diary on September 12 that "it would bring the greatest odium on my Father—it would not be tolerated at a period especially when our troops were so perpetually victorious. O how My heart ached that day."[23]

In fact, the criticism had started as soon as Prevost ordered the retreat. On the battlefield in Plattsburgh, seasoned generals Robinson, Brisbane, and Power were shocked. All had served under Wellington and been called by the duke the finest of their rank.[24] Commanding the forces that had successfully forded the Saranac River and begun their march to take the American forts in Plattsburgh, Robinson and Power were stunned, they and their men believing that victory was at hand and would be theirs shortly. Their anger at Prevost's decision to withdraw was fueled by the negative opinion that many already held of him. In the first place, most of the officers and men did not want to be in Canada after their service on the Iberian Peninsula. They also resented being commanded by Prevost, whom they considered to be an overly officious administrative general with little combat experience.

In a long letter to Anthony Merry on September 22, General Robinson described his part in the land battle. Praising the navy and

Captain Downie, Robinson described "our disgraceful and unfortunate expedition to Plattsburg" and criticized Prevost's conduct without mentioning him by name. He claimed that Prevost did not have a clear plan of attack and that he and his staff had also failed to gather necessary intelligence. When they began their march on September 11, Robinson and his men did not know the precise location of the fords across the Saranac or the distance to the enemy redoubts, "*nor had they guides of any kind.*" The general also blamed Prevost for delaying his departure on the morning of the battle. Then, once underway, his forces had lost a full hour when they got lost and had to retrace their steps because Prevost's staff did not know the correct route.[25]

According to Robinson, once he had finally reached the ford, his troops formed and attacked. Six companies "dashed down a very steep and high bank, and forded the river like so many foxhounds, driving the Doodles in all directions." Once on the other side, they halted to wait for the remaining troops to cross. It was at this moment that an aide-de-camp from Prevost arrived with the order to "retire immediately" because the *Confiance* and the *Linnet* had surrendered. "Never was anything like the disappointment expressed in every countenance. The advance was within shot and full view of the redoubts, and in one hour they must have been ours." The army then retreated "in a most precipitate and disgraceful manner" as it destroyed its guns, ammunition, and supplies in the process. Robinson was disgusted. "I am sick at heart, everything I see and hear is discouraging. . . . The departments are all jumbled together, and nothing goes right but in the commissariat." The general also observed that the navy had been "roused to the highest pitch of indignation and do not scruple saying, it was sacrificed at the shrine of indecision and a total want of judgment." Specifically, the squadron had been promised that the American shore fortifications would be attacked once the squadron rounded Cumberland Head, but that did not happen. Although it did not criticize Prevost by name, Robinson's letter painted a depressing picture of poor preparation, mismanagement, and bad judgment by the commander in chief of the offensive. When he received the letter in London, Merry shared it with Lord Bathurst.[26]

Initially, Prevost did not make any special efforts to defend himself or protect his standing with the government in London. Both of his dispatches on September 11 and 12 were routine explanations of the battle and his decision to withdraw. He praised the "intrepid valor" of Captain Downie but explained that his own hopes "for complete success" were "blasted" by a "combination . . . of unfortunate events, to which naval warfare is peculiarly exposed." Because the surrender of the *Confiance* and the *Linnet* deprived him of the "co-operation of the fleet, without which the further prosecution of the service was become impracticable," Prevost did not "hesitate to arrest the course of the troops advancing to the attack, because the most complete success would have been unavailing and the possession of the enemy's works offered no advantage to compensate for the loss we must have sustained in acquiring possession of them."[27]

The next day Prevost wrote again to London to explain briefly that "no Offensive Operations could be carried out within the Enemy's Territory for the destruction of his Naval Establishment without Naval Support." Since the "disastrous" naval battle had denied him "the only means by which I could avail myself of any advantage I might gain," Prevost judged it "highly imprudent as well as hazardous" to continue the land assault. Under the circumstances, he declared, he had sacrificed his "own fame by [not] gratifying the ardor of the troops in persevering in the attack" and instead had bowed to "the more substantial interest of my country by withdrawing the Army."[28]

On September 16 from Montreal, Prevost repeated his reasoning to Lieutenant General Gordon Drummond explaining that he had intended "to establish the Army at Plattsburg and to detach from thence a Brigade for the destruction of Vergennes & its Naval establishment." The "melancholy fate" of Downie's squadron "blasted these intentions and compelled me to bring back the Troops nearer to their supplies."[29] In these explanations Prevost was referring directly to his June 3 orders in which Lord Bathurst had specified that one of the two main objectives of the offensive from Canada was to be the destruction of the U.S. "naval establishment" on Lakes Ontario and Champlain and the occupation of territory along Lake Champlain. But these instructions also explicitly admonished Prevost to take care always "not [to] expose His Majesty's Forces to being cut off by too extended a line of advance." Accordingly, the naval action having failed on Lake Champlain, he had hastened to withdraw the troops rather than endanger his supply and communication lines.[30]

On September 22 Prevost reiterated the reasoning for his abrupt withdrawal in a "private" letter to Bathurst. He repeated that his operations on land depended heavily on naval success on the lake. Accordingly, the disastrous defeat in Cumberland Bay rendered a continued attack on shore "highly imprudent, as well as hazardous." The roads were becoming nearly impassable, and the "Enemy's Militia was raising En Masse around me." Had he continued to fight and not succeeded, "the destruction of a great part of my Troops must have been the consequence." His strategic retreat, however, had left his army "uncrippled" for the continued defense and security of Canada.[31]

Meanwhile, soon after the battle Commodore Yeo began to collect evidence to exonerate the navy of blame. The first report to reach him from Lieutenant Colonel Edward Brenton, Prevost's civil secretary, was incomplete and full of mistakes with respect to casualties. It blamed no one for the campaign's failure, but other accounts from Captain Pring, Lieutenant Robertson, and the prebattle correspondence between Prevost and Downie pointed the finger of blame at the governor in chief. Based on the information that he collected, Yeo blamed Prevost's command of the army for the defeat in letters to the British Admiralty on September 16 and 24 as well as subsequent letters and documents to London.[32] The commodore was hardly a neutral observer. As commander of British naval forces on the northern lakes, Yeo had responsibility for the squadron on Lake Champlain and was painfully aware that he personally had continually declined Prevost's requests for more men and naval resources there. He also had made the last-minute decision to replace Captain Fisher with Captain Downie, a stranger to the officers and crew he would command and the waters of the lake on which he was to sail.

The heart of Yeo's case was based on material that he had received from Pring, commander of the *Linnet* and the second in command of the squadron. Pring wrote to Yeo on September 12 and 17 and included a report from Robertson, who had replaced Downie in command of the *Confiance* after the captain had been killed. In his reports Yeo blamed the naval defeat on the actions of Prevost for several reasons. First, once Downie had commenced his naval attack in Cumberland Bay, the army had not immediately attacked and taken the American batteries in Plattsburgh. Second, in his impatience to begin the attack, Prevost had pressured Downie into action before the *Confiance* was prepared to meet the enemy. In fact, in one of his letters Yeo charged that Downie "was urged, even goaded on to his fate" by Prevost. Third, the commodore charged that even after the British squadron had surrendered, the day might not have been lost had Prevost pressed his attack into the town. With the U.S. squadron momentarily victorious but disabled, the British ships might have been retaken by driving off the remaining American gunboats.[33]

Although their effect in London was not immediate, Yeo's charges against Prevost planted fertile seeds in the Admiralty and played a critical role in undermining the governor's credibility and reputation. Prevost himself seems not to have understood that a naval campaign to undermine him was underway. In early October he visited Yeo at Kingston, where the massive 112-gun HMS *St. Lawrence* was about to sail. There, Prevost and Yeo apparently did not discuss the events of September 11 in detail, nor did the commodore apparently question him about the issues he had raised in writing to the Admiralty.[34] In December Prevost explained to Bathurst that he was unable to explain the actions of those naval officers "who did not do their duty on the 11th of September." In addition to the commander of HMS *Chub*, Lieutenant McGhie, who had disappeared several days after the battle, Lieutenant Raynham, the commander of the British gunboats, had also deserted. Yet Prevost informed Bathurst that he now suspected that "a desire exists" by the navy to "stifle Enquiry . . . since it has been correctly ascertained that our Squadron upon that occasion was superior to that of the Enemy in every respect."[35]

In Canada the governor in chief was under fire from various public and private sources. In fact, he was already unpopular with the English-speaking minority in Lower Canada because of actions that he had taken since 1811. After his appointment in September 1811, Prevost had worked to conciliate the French-speaking majority in Lower Canada by reversing some of the policies of his predecessor, James Craig, who had served from 1807 to 1811.

Known to some as the "Anglophile Governor," Craig had strongly aligned with the English minority in its conflict with the French majority, which he deemed disloyal. While the latter controlled the popularly elected Assembly, the British minority controlled the Legislative and Executive Councils. In his efforts to suppress French nationalism, Craig dissolved the Assembly on several occasions, arrested the owners of the leading French-speaking newspaper, and cancelled militia commissions. But his actions only fueled a burning anti-English resentment. In fact, most of the French-speaking population was loyal to their current government. Wanting nothing to do with the United States, they sought simply to live their lives in British-ruled Canada in a French Canadian manner.[36]

Craig also took sides in a religious dispute between the French-speaking Catholic majority and the English-speaking Anglican minority. At issue was a battle between Anglican bishop James Mountain and his counterpart, Catholic bishop Joseph-Octave Plessis. Objecting to Plessis, Mountain campaigned to reverse the London government's decision to recognize Plessis as the Catholic bishop of Canada. In 1813 he complained to Bathurst about the formal recognition of "a religion which every man of unfettered judgment admits to be equally unfavorable to morality, to industry, and to improvement."[37]

When Prevost became governor in chief in 1811, he began to reverse Craig's policies, actions for which he would become known as the "Francophile Governor." He believed that the "system of coercion practiced by my predecessor" undermined the security of Canada. Most controversial was his relationship with Bishop Plessis, whom he befriended. Prevost secured a large salary increase for him and gained official confirmation of his bishopric. As a result, as war between England and the United States loomed, the Catholic Church in Canada became a firm supporter of Prevost, his militia and currency laws, and the war effort.[38]

In retrospect, Prevost's administrative policies were generally wise and farsighted. Certainly serving Canada well during the War of 1812, they have been well regarded subsequently by most historians. They also won the support of the French Canadian majority in Lower Canada, who remained loyal to the government. In the first year of the conflict, Bishop Plessis praised the war effort and particularly the "Commander in Chief whose indefatigable activity . . . affability . . . [and] impartiality manifest to all subjects of his Majesty in this Province that they have but one and the same interest, that of the common defence." A letter in Montreal's *Le Spectateur* noted that when war came, "French Canadians flew to arms" and praised the leadership of the governor in chief. "He has known how, in winning the trust and affection of French Canadians, to develop his defensive resources and capabilities in a manner beyond the power of his predecessor. Up to now his efforts have met with steady success, brilliant victory have constantly followed our just cause and have disgraced our enemies."[39]

Unsurprisingly, Prevost's policies were very unpopular with the English-speaking minority, some of whom were outspoken and persistent in their opposition. Most prominent was Bishop Mountain, but there were others as well. Moreover, Prevost's actions during the war increased the number of his detractors. Some of his critics, such as opposition newspapers, were open and direct; others were circumspect but effective.

One well-connected critic was Alicia Cockburn, sister-in-law of Admiral George Cockburn and wife of Lieutenant General Francis Cockburn of the Canadian Fencibles. With her husband away on duty, she spent most of the war in Quebec or Montreal, where she gathered information and wrote letters criticizing Prevost. In a letter to her cousin Charles Sandys in June 1814, she reported that "all is bustle" with the arrival of troops from Europe but noted, "if I commanded, I would move it a *little nearer the enemy.*—however there are some worthy people who have the happy knack of discovering *danger* long before it approaches." Although she did not mention him by name, Prevost's caution reminded her of an old poem:

> He who fights & runs away,
> May live to fight another day,
> But he who is in Battle slain,
> Will never rise to fight again.—[40]

In the aftermath of Plattsburgh, Cockburn wrote a confidential letter in which she observed that the "recent disgraceful business of Plattsburg has so completely irritated the feelings of the whole army, that it is in a state almost amounting to mutiny." She also accused Prevost of previously making "his own story good in England" through "art and deception . . . to blind the eyes of Ministers at home." But now desperate, he was "sending home creatures who are dependent on him" to tell his story. Recently, a Mr. Brenton, "a low, dirty fellow," had departed secretly for England "to make as good a story for Sir George as he can."[41]

For her part, Cockburn collected and furnished Lord Arthur Somerset, who was visiting Canada to investigate the matter, with confidential documents about the Plattsburgh campaign, hoping that he would reveal the truth after his return to England. She claimed that "the popular voice in Canada" was "loud and clamorous" on the matter. "Had any man with common abilities been at the head of this Government . . . we must long ago have taught the Yankees submission, & been at Peace. Such is the decided opinion of every military man in the Province, whether his rank be high or low, so glaring are the state of affairs at this moment." Moreover, the "civil Government of the Province, is in a state no less deplorable than the military." If we must "'fight it out,'" we must have "another Chief, 'one who has valour to assert our cause'—not a mean-spirited, ignorant man who sprung from the lowest origin, (for his Father was a Drummer in the Swiss service)."[42]

Cockburn's criticism was private, but her sentiments were shared by English-speaking Canadians and by the press in Lower Canada. Newspapers, including the *Montreal Herald*, carried accounts and letters that condemned Prevost. Under the pseudonyms "Veritas" and "Nerva," attacks appeared in the paper. According to one historian, "the violence of the press in array against him [Prevost] knew no bounds." These articles charged Prevost at Plattsburgh with "having on that memorable expedition, sacrificed the flotilla, and as far as in him lay, disgraced the army under his command."[43] The *Montreal Herald* also carried a long letter on the expedition to Plattsburgh, stating that it "has ended in such disastrous disappointment as to excite a degree of astonishment and sensibility, that surpasses all past experience here." Although not mentioning Prevost by name, the author, "An Englishman," stated it "appears fair and candid, that what is said should reach the ears of the person blamed for the failure of all our expectations." In the indictment's list of particulars, the author repeated all of the same charges against Prevost that had been identified by Yeo and forwarded to the Admiralty in London.[44]

Questioning the loyalty of Prevost, who had been born in colonial New Jersey, one letter in a Halifax newspaper claimed that the governor's biography "would occupy but a small part of a very small page." The writer asked "if there ever was a worse conducted, or a more disastrous War than ours in Canada"? Another writer asked, "is it to be wondered at that where ability and experience are not, that success should be wanting? And that discomfiture should be the result of miserable mismanagement."[45]

The public frustration with and criticism of Prevost in Canada soon found its way across the Atlantic. After news of the disaster at Plattsburgh reached London, criticism of Prevost followed quickly in the press. Several letters criticizing him appeared in the *Morning*

Post of London, one of which noted, "We . . . perceive that Sir George Prevost is not entirely popular in Canada." In late October another London paper carried a scathing and mistake-filled account of the governor in chief.[46]

Shortly after the initial news of the battle had reached London, accusations from the British generals at Plattsburgh and Commodore Yeo also began to arrive. The Liverpool government was shocked by the defeat on Lake Champlain and retreat from Plattsburgh because it confidently expected a total victory. Now the depressing news from North America increased political criticism of the government's conduct of the war. If the conflict in North America was to be won, it would require another campaign season in 1815, meaning higher government deficits and the maintenance of high taxes. In the search for explanations for the stunning defeat, attention inevitably focused on Prevost, who lacked strong defenders in the government and a compelling defense of his conduct during the planning and execution of the campaign.

Although he recognized his political weakness in Lower Canada, Prevost was now in a vulnerable position in London as well. On October 15, soon after he received word of the defeat at Plattsburgh, Bathurst wrote to Wellington in Paris for advice. On October 30 the duke replied: "It is very obvious to me that you must remove Sir George Prevost. I see he has gone to war about trifles with the general officers I sent him, which are certainly the best of their rank in the army; and his subsequent failure and distress will be aggravated by that circumstance; and will probably with the usual fairness of the public be attributed to it." Although he recommended that Prevost be replaced, Wellington later defended the decision to withdraw from Plattsburgh. "I admire all that has been done in America, as far as I understand it generally. Whether Sir George Prevost was right or wrong in his decision at Lake Champlain is more than I can tell; but of this I am very certain, he must have retired to Kingston [Montreal] after our fleet was beaten, and I am inclined to believe he was right." The duke believed that "Prevost will justify his misfortunes, which . . . I am quite certain are not what the Americans have represented them to be."[47]

In November, when Liverpool and Bathurst decided to remove Prevost, they based their decision on Yeo's version of battle. On the eighteenth, in words that mirrored the commodore's charges, Liverpool explained to Wellington that Downie "never would have attacked the American fleet at anchor off Plattsburgh if he [Prevost] had not promised to attack the fort at the same time; that if he fulfilled his engagement, the misfortune to the fleet would not have occurred." Even after the squadron had surrendered, it might "have been retaken if the fort had been captured, as it was some hours before the Americans, in their crippled state, were able to take possession of the British ships."[48]

Bathurst then updated Lord Henry Goulburn, the undersecretary of state for war and the colonies and one of the peace commissioners at Ghent, of this decision. Goulburn replied that he was "glad Sir G. Prevost is recalled. The affair at Plattsburgh is to me still unaccountable, and I am, though perhaps unjustly, disposed to give weight to the charges brought forward by Sir J. Yeo." At the same time, he cautioned that any replacement would have a difficult time in Canada because of the differences that existed between "officers of the naval and military service there."[49]

Prevost remained completely unaware of his removal, learning of it only in March 1815, when his replacement arrived in Canada. Shocked, he wrapped up his affairs quickly and was on his way back to Britain the following month. Before departing, he was praised in a resolution from the Assembly and given a full-plate service. Since he believed that he had conducted himself in an entirely responsible and defensible manner, Prevost was confident that he would be acquitted in a formal court-martial. Unfortunately, the court-martial scheduled for early 1816 was never held; Prevost died in January before it convened.[50]

In London and in Washington, the British and American governments reacted similarly to the first reports of the actions at Lake Champlain and Plattsburgh. Having initially underestimated the importance of the events of September 11, both believed that the U.S. victory would not shorten the war. Instead, both the Madison administration and the Liverpool government resolved to continue the conflict, which they foresaw lasting at least another year. But in deciding to replace Prevost in Canada, Bathurst had opened the door to a serious reassessment of the war effort by the cabinet.

CHAPTER 6

REPERCUSSIONS

LONDON AND GHENT

In September 1814 at the Flemish town of Ghent in the Netherlands, the prospects for an honorable peace settlement for the United States seemed unlikely. Since it took news from North America roughly five weeks to reach them, the U.S. peace commissioners had very few recent military reports, and what they had received was not encouraging. Actual negotiations, which had started on August 8, had not gone well. The American and British delegations were far apart, with little common ground between them. "It appears now certain that they [the British] have more serious and dangerous objects in view," wrote Albert Gallatin to Secretary of State Monroe. "It is now evident that Great Britain intends to strengthen and aggrandize herself in North America."[1] Given the situation, the Americans expected that negotiations would soon break off.

The pessimism of the American delegation reflected the great disparity between the positions of the United States and Great Britain. The Americans were in a tenuous military and political situation at home and could expect no foreign assistance.[2] In contrast, Britain was in a commanding position, which was manifested in the confident, demanding, and expansive mood of its government. In the aftermath of vanquishing Napoleon, Britain had emerged as the dominant power of Europe. It now focused seriously for the first time on the war in North America. In addition to tightening the blockade on the U.S. coast, the government had sent thousands of reinforcements to Canada for offensive operations to secure territorial footholds on the Great Lakes, Lake Champlain, and Maine. It had sent a powerful diversionary flotilla to invade and attack targets along Chesapeake Bay. It also planned to attack New Orleans and the U.S. gulf coast.

By 1814, Prime Minister Lord Liverpool had been in power since 1812. His government included Foreign Secretary Viscount Castlereagh and War and Colonial Secretary Lord Bathurst. This capable team agreed on the need to chastise the Americans militarily and to extract real concessions from them in the peace settlement. As foreign secretary, Lord Castlereagh had managed diplomatic efforts to end the war. He prepared the initial instructions in July for the British peace commissioners and then in August personally delivered revised instructions in Ghent.[3] From there he traveled to Paris and Vienna, where he would play a major role in the Congress of Vienna. As a result of Castlereagh's extended absence from London, Lord Bathurst assumed primary responsibility for overseeing the ongoing negotiations as well as managing military operations in North America. For military advice, the government also relied on the expertise of its minister to France, the Duke of Wellington, who had been victorious against Napoleon's forces in Spain.

Shortly after peace negotiations had begun, the Liverpool government expanded its territorial objectives. The large amphibious squadron planned for the Gulf of Mexico and New Orleans had originally been conceived as a diversionary operation. Now in early September, it assumed two more-threatening goals. First, the operation was to command the mouth of the Mississippi River so as to deprive the extensive American back settlements of their communications with the sea. Second, the army was "to occupy some important and valuable possession by the restoration of which we may improve the conditions of peace, or which may entitle us to exact its cession as the price of peace." Major General Robert Ross, who was to command the land forces of the operation, was instructed to encourage the local inhabitants to revolt from the United States without making any formal commitments to them. In other words, the future of Louisiana now hung in the military balance.[4]

The war against the United States enjoyed strong public and journalistic support in Britain. Since the fall of Napoleon, the press had been demanding that the Americans be severely punished for the apostasy of having supported the French. In the words of the London *Times*, British terms "may be couched in a single word, *Submission*." Another London paper insisted that the Americans not be "left in a condition to repeat their insults, injuries, and wrongs, whenever the situation of Europe should encourage them to resume their arms." Territorial concessions were seen as the price of peace.

A widely circulated pamphlet demanded revision of the Canadian border, American exclusion from the Great Lakes, the creation of a permanent Indian buffer state in the Northwest, the cession of New Orleans, and the exclusion of U.S. ships from British colonial ports.[5]

In Ghent Gallatin had already recognized that Britain's "true and immediate object is New Orleans." Since it was the "most distant and weakest point" in the Union, it could not be retaken by the United States "without great difficulty" if it was successfully occupied by the enemy: "there is no possession which . . . both in a political and in a commercial view, they would be more desirous of holding." Moreover, if the primary British offensive in Canada was "less successful than they expect, New Orleans would be made a set-off, and its restitution to depend on our compliance with their demands in the North."[6]

Given the overwhelming superiority of its forces, the Liverpool government confidently anticipated victories on Lake Ontario, Lake Champlain, and Chesapeake Bay. Based on its military buildup and the expectation of decisive victories, the government had changed its diplomatic strategy in the summer of 1814. In December 1813, before the war had ended in Europe, the British had been willing to conclude a separate peace with the United States based on the principle of *"status quo ante bellum* without involving in such Treaty any decision on the points in dispute at the commencement of hostilities [that is, impressments and neutral rights]."[7] The proposal was also to include a definite date by which the United States would have to accept or refuse the offer. But since face-to-face negotiations had not yet begun, the opportunity for a settlement passed abruptly with Napoleon's defeat.

Now the British sought to impose a harsh peace that would protect their interests in North America and guarantee long-term security for Upper and Lower Canada. Drafted by Castlereagh, the instructions to the British delegation were general rather than specific. They authorized the commissioners to discuss but not abandon the practice of impressment and to include an "adequate Arrangement" with Indians in the Northwest as a "sine qua non of Peace." They were also to discuss redrawing the Canada–U.S. border, which had been "very hastily and improvidently framed" at the end of the American Revolution, and to insist that the Americans furnish an equivalent for the retention of their Canadian fishing privileges, which had been abrogated by the war. Simply stated, these instructions called for the creation of an Indian buffer state from U.S. territory in the Northwest and the revision of the international border to give Canada control of both sides of the Saint Lawrence River and part of eastern Maine. The British also expected to eliminate the American privilege to fish in Canadian waters and to dry their catches on Canadian shores while allowing the British to maintain their existing treaty right to navigate the Mississippi River freely.[8]

In the late summer of 1814, the British government was not in a hurry to come to terms. Having committed extensive resources to North America and unleashed a multifront offensive, it wanted victories in those operations to shape any peace treaty. Accordingly, the Liverpool government intended to wait until news of the expected victories arrived from overseas. Having previously agreed to negotiations at Ghent, the British moved slowly to begin actual talks. The five-man U.S. delegation had arrived in Belgium by the end of June, but London postponed appointing its commissioners, keeping the Americans waiting for six weeks during the summer of 1814.

The Liverpool government also believed that given its strong diplomatic and military position, it could readily impose its terms on the Americans. "If the campaign in Canada should be as successful as our military preparations would lead us to expect," the prime minister predicted confidently that there would be no need to make concessions.[9] Once news of British victories arrived, the Americans would be forced either to break off negotiations or accept London's terms. Since it would be one sided, the conference at Ghent would not require difficult, complicated, or prolonged negotiations. Accordingly, the Foreign Office did not send a top-flight delegation because it continued to be most concerned about the diplomatic situation in Europe. Indeed, when Foreign Minister Castlereagh left England in August for Paris and the conference at Vienna, he passed through Ghent but did not linger there.

The three-man British delegation was individually and collectively inferior to the Americans both in terms of its diplomatic experience and its ability to negotiate.[10] Fifty-seven-year-old Lord James Gambier was a career naval officer who had risen to become admiral of the fleet. His long career included many assignments, most notably the bombardment of Copenhagen in 1807. A strong defender of impressment, he was an expert on British naval practices but neither an experienced diplomat nor an effective negotiator.

Dr. William Adams had considerable expertise in maritime law, but he did not play an important role in the peace talks. Although he was the youngest member of the delegation, Henry Goulburn emerged as its leader. He was a rising thirty-year-old politician who was the undersecretary for war and the colonies. At the outset of negotiations, the undistinguished quality of the British delegation did not seem to be important because of the strength of the British position. In addition, unlike the Americans, who were far removed from Washington, the British could readily request additional instructions from London.

The U.S. delegation also waited for news from North America, although the prospects seemed bleak. Headed by John Quincy Adams, the well-balanced team included Henry Clay, Albert Gallatin, James Bayard, and Jonathan Russell. By any measure, it was one of the strongest diplomatic delegations ever to represent the United States. The forty-seven-year-old Adams was a brilliant man and experienced diplomat. Under the tutelage of his father, John Adams, he had spent much of his youth abroad in Europe. After receiving his degree from Harvard, Adams became a lawyer but soon entered politics. He had held a number of diplomatic posts, including most recently minister to Russia. Ten years younger than Adams, Clay had twice served as speaker of the House of Representatives. A shrewd and immensely talented politician, the Kentuckian was also a fierce nationalist and a leading War Hawk in 1812. Gallatin was a naturalized U.S. citizen who had been born in Switzerland. To some observers, his manners seemed more European than American, an observation that pleased him. An exceptionally talented individual with a first-rate financial mind, he had risen in the Republican Party during the 1790s, serving capably as secretary of the Treasury in both the Jefferson and Madison administrations. He also had important personal connections in England and Europe and was genuinely respected by British officials. Although they were lesser persons by comparison, Bayard and Russell were both able men. Bayard was a distinguished lawyer and moderate Federalist from Delaware, and Russell a Republican from Rhode Island.[11]

While the U.S. delegation presented a unified front in the negotiations, the strength of their individual personalities created considerable disagreements and tensions behind the scenes. Adams and Clay were aggressive and stubborn individuals with strong opinions. Gallatin held equally strong views but adeptly eased tensions or repaired breeches within the group. Although they disagreed frequently and spoke critically of one another in private, the Americans maintained public unity and never wavered in their determination to defend U.S. rights and not compromise their principles to their adversaries.

Their impressive talents notwithstanding, the Americans faced a daunting and dismal challenge when the talks finally began on August 8 on neutral ground in the Hotel des Pays-Bas, where the very first session demonstrated that the British wanted to impose a vindictive peace. After the initial meetings, Gallatin suspected that they sought control of Lakes Ontario and Erie, the cession of Detroit, the creation of an Indian buffer state, and possibly even the cession of New Orleans and Louisiana; in short, Britain intended to "strengthen and aggrandize herself in North America."[12] Clay and Bayard were of like mind. Without the threat of interference from any other European power, predicted Bayard, Britain will make the effort "to crush Us altogether and if that be impracticable to inflict such wounds as will put a stop to our growth or at least retard it." Clay thought that these initial demands might represent merely "an experiment on us" in the hope "that they will strike some signal blow, during the present campaign." But four days later, he too was dismayed and confided that the "prospect of peace has disappeared."[13] By the end of August, ever the pessimist, Adams was convinced that the British demands "opened to us the alternative of a long, expensive and sangwinary War, or of submission to disgraceful conditions, and sacrifices little short of Independence itself."[14]

The delegation had two sets of instructions, one drafted in 1813 and another in January 1814. In 1813 Secretary of State Monroe had initially authorized negotiation on issues of maritime law but no compromise on impressment. In January 1814 he had reiterated this position. "This degrading practice must cease; our flag must protect the crew, or the United States cannot consider themselves an independent nation."[15] Monroe had also authorized the commissioners to try to acquire Canada by explaining to the British that both nations would benefit by the "transfer of the upper parts and even the whole of Canada to the United States."[16] Given its weak bargaining position, the American team never presented this proposal during the talks. Then, just as negotiations began, the delegation received additional instructions that granted discretion to abandon or compromise on impressment as an issue rather than insist that the British end the practice.[17]

On the first day of talks, following introductions and formalities, Goulburn explained that the British delegation was authorized to discuss four issues: impressment, the Indians and their borders, the Canadian border, and the privilege of Americans to fish in Canadian waters and dry their catch on Canadian shores. He then asked whether the Americans had instructions on these issues. They deferred their answer until the next day, responding then that they had instructions on impressment and the Canadian border questions but not on the Indian or fisheries issues. The Americans did, however, say that they were willing to discuss these and other matters. Yet in the conversation that followed, when the commissioners explained their government's intention to create an Indian buffer state between Canada and the United States in the Northwest, the Americans refused to even discuss such a proposal.

The British then suggested that the talks be suspended to allow time for them to receive specific instructions from London. Castlereagh soon sent additional details to his initial directions. On August 14 he told the delegation to propose an Indian border state whose boundaries would be those fixed by the Treaty of Greenville (1795). The commissioners were to propose the "rectification" of the Canadian border by the American cession of Fort Niagara and Sackets Harbor. They were also to seek the cession of land in Maine to permit the construction of a road from Quebec to Halifax as well as territory in the west to permit Canadian access to the upper Mississippi. Moreover, the United States was to be prohibited from maintaining any fortifications or naval forces on any of the Great Lakes. With these revised instructions in hand, Castlereagh reached Ghent on August 18. After meeting with his commissioners, the foreign secretary departed for Paris on the twentieth.[18]

In talks the following day, the British presented the Indian buffer state as a sine qua non of peace but did not similarly insist on their Great Lakes proposal. When Goulburn finished reading his proposal, Gallatin asked what was to happen to the roughly 100,000 Americans living within the borders of the proposed Indian buffer. To this, Dr. Adams responded simply that they would have to shift for themselves. The next day the British followed up by sending an official note outlining what they had stated verbally the previous day.

The American situation seemed grim indeed. Since the terms presented by the British were completely unacceptable, four of the five delegates believed that the U.S. response would end the peace talks. Only Clay saw any reason for hope, thinking that the proposal might be a probing tactic or bluff.[19] Nevertheless, negotiations seemed likely to terminate soon. Since the British proposals, particularly the idea of an Indian buffer state as a sine quo non, were completely unacceptable, the Americans decided that they would respond formally for the record. Expecting that their response would end the talks, they did not request additional instructions from Washington. Instead, they simply packaged and dispatched the written British proposals to the United States.

Initially drafted by John Quincy Adams, the American response was thoroughly revised after the other commissioners sharply criticized it. Heated discussion produced an unequivocal response. It dismissed the British proposals as not founded on the "usual basis of negotiation" of either uti possidetis (actual possession of territory) or of status quo antebellum (territory occupied before the war). Their demands were "above all dishonorable to the United States in demanding from them to abandon territory and a portion of their citizens to admit a foreign interference in their domestic concerns, and to cease to exercise their natural rights on their own shores and in their own waters. A treaty concluded on such terms would be but an armistice." In response, they proposed the simple end of hostilities, with both parties relinquishing any territory that they had taken.[20]

Here the talks were suspended while the British negotiators waited for another response from London to the American note. Both delegations assumed the peace talks to be at an end. But unbeknown to the Americans, the British had exceeded their instructions. In fact, Castlereagh had not insisted on the creation of an Indian buffer state, as presented by Goulburn as a sine qua non, but only on adequate guarantees of future security for Britain's Indian allies. When he learned of the position the delegation had presented, Liverpool wrote to Castlereagh, "Our commissioners had certainly taken a very erroneous view of our policy." Thereafter, the Foreign Office did not hesitate to chastise or correct its delegation, which was now on a short leash. Whenever the Americans rejected or disagreed with a position, their counterparts simply referred the matter to London for a decision. As they tried to cope with American intransigence, the British commissioners became impatient for good news from North America. In early September Goulburn was disappointed by "Prevost's indisposition to attempt anything." "I wish Prevost may quickly do something worthy of the force now placed under his command," he wrote, "a success in that quarter . . . much assists us in our present negotiations."[21]

Officials in London wanted the negotiations to continue while awaiting military news from North America. They still had no word on the offensives on Chesapeake Bay, Lake Ontario, the coast of Maine, or Lake Champlain. Moreover, if talks were to end prematurely, the Liverpool government did not want them to cease on this note. The British proposals then on the table painted the war in North America as one of conquest against the United States, not as one to protect Canada. If negotiations had been allowed to break off at this point, noted Liverpool, "I am satisfied that the war would have become quite popular in America."[22]

The prime minister's strategy, then, was to prolong the negotiations pending favorable military news. "If our commander does his duty," wrote Liverpool, "I am persuaded we shall have acquired by our arms every point on the Canadian frontier which we ought to insist on keeping." From early September through mid-October, the British retreated from their demands on the Indian buffer state and the removal of U.S. forts and naval vessels from the Great Lakes. The Liverpool government first softened and then abandoned its position on both issues.[23] On September 16 a note instructed the commissioners to drop the demand for exclusive control of the Great Lakes. They were also directed to insist only that the Indians be included in the final treaty, not guaranteed their own buffer state. When the Americans responded with an offer of amnesty for the Indians who had fought with Britain, the British at first rejected it but then suggested an alternative that would merely restore the Indians to their prewar situation.[24] By mid-October, the Americans agreed to this proposal, which effectively removed the Indian issue from the negotiations. Critical in this process was news from North America. At the end of September, word reached Ghent that in July the United States and Indian tribes in the Northwest had signed a peace treaty in which the latter had agreed to switch sides and fight against their erstwhile British allies.[25] This accord obviously weakened London's allegiance to the Indians and removed any sense of obligation that they be included in a final peace settlement.

Although they retreated on these two issues, the British continued to harbor territorial objectives. The Liverpool government expected to redraw the Canadian border to reverse the mistakes that had been made in the peace treaty of 1783. These demands included, but were not limited to, the cession of eastern Maine, control of the southern bank of the Saint Lawrence River to Lake Ontario, and the cession of Fort Niagara and Sackets Harbor as well as Michilimackinac and the islands in Passamaquoddy Bay.

The military situation in North America seemed sure to strengthen these demands. "Our prospects in America are I think good," predicted Bathurst.[26] Then at the end of September, the anticipated good news began to arrive. British forces had occupied eastern Maine and the USS *Adams* had been destroyed. Nantucket had capitulated. On the twenty-seventh reports arrived that the force under General Ross had landed in Maryland, routed American defenders at Bladensburg, and captured Washington, D.C., burning several public and private buildings before withdrawing. A few days later came word that Alexandria had surrendered to avoid similar destruction. British politicians and newspapers exalted as they anticipated more good news from Chesapeake Bay and Canada.

Although the Liverpool government cheered the news, Bathurst informed their delegation that he did not intend to use these victories to increase their demands. Indeed, London expected that news of the capture of Washington would reduce American intransigence at Ghent. In fact, it had the opposite immediate effect. When they read the news, the U.S. commissioners were outraged at the destruction of civilian buildings and private property. In both Ghent and the United States, the attack on Washington had stirred American resolve and rejuvenated American patriotism.[27]

Thus, in early October the British, who had refused to insist explicitly at the outset upon either uti possidetis or status quo antebellum as the basis for peace, now decided to press for a peace based on uti possidetis. According to the *London Courier*, the government's position was to make peace, "but it must be on condition that America has not a foot of land on the waters of the St. Lawrence, . . . no settlement on the Lakes, . . . [and] no renewal of the treaties of 1783 and 1794." On September 23 Liverpool had explained that his government would now stand firm on its demands. It had reached "the utmost justifiable point in concession, and if they are so unreasonable as to reject our proposals, we have nothing to do but to fight it out. The military accounts from America are on the whole satisfactory."[28] He and Bathurst clearly intended to translate Prevost's military victories into U.S. territorial cessions at the conference table.[29]

Expecting additional good news to follow shortly, the British continued to prolong the talks. Let the Americans "feast in the mean time upon Washington," Liverpool advised. By October 10, the prime minister confidently predicted more victories. Prevost "has a noble army, and ought certainly to be in Possession at this time of Sacket's Harbour, and of Plattsburg," wrote Liverpool. According to Commissioner Russell, this confidence further weakened the U.S. position.[30]

At this point, the Americans in Ghent had little to show for their efforts. Having effectively abandoned their position on impressment, they had managed only to beat back proposals to create an Indian buffer state and remove American arms from the Great Lakes. But with the British remaining determined to readjust the Canadian border, it seemed that there was little that they could do but tenaciously refuse to accept such demands. Moreover, the news from North America was bad. In addition to the debacle at Washington, the Americans knew that eastern Maine had been occupied, the *Adams* had been burned, and Fort Mackinac remained under British control. There were also reports that Plattsburgh had fallen.[31] Even Clay, normally the most optimistic member of the delegation, was discouraged and angered that "a set of pirates and incendiaries should have been permitted to pollute our soil[,] conflagrate our Capital, and return unpunished to their ships." He feared worse was yet to come. "I tremble indeed whenever I take up a late News paper. Hope alone sustains me."[32]

Meanwhile, on October 17 word reached London that the British fleet in the Chesapeake had attacked but then retreated from Baltimore. In the fighting General Ross had been killed. Although not as decisive as Washington, some interpreted the battle as another British victory. The headline in the *London Sun* announced, "AMERICAN ARMY DEFEATED NEAR BALTIMORE—GENERAL ROSS KILLED—REEMBARKATION OF THE EXPEDITION." When he received the news at Ghent, Goulburn referred to "our brilliant success" even though it "did not terminate in the capture of the town."[33]

Accompanying the news from Baltimore was word from northern New York. As expected, the formidable army under Prevost had invaded the state and occupied Plattsburgh against light resistance. But then on September 11, an American squadron had defeated and captured the British naval force on Lake Champlain. In the immediate aftermath, Prevost had abruptly withdrawn his army from Plattsburgh and returned to Canada. Initial reaction to this surprising news in London was mixed. Some believed that the retreat might be only a temporary setback. "The affair at Plattsburgh is but a feather in the general scale," announced the *London Sun* on October 19. But it quickly became clear that Lake Champlain and Plattsburgh were not feathers. Later, another newspaper referred to Plattsburgh as a "disaster," while the *Times* labeled it "a defeat still more disastrous" than the Battle of Lake Erie in 1813. "This is a lamentable event to the civilized world," exaggerated the *Times* on the nineteenth. "The present [American] government must be displaced, or it will sooner or later plant its poisoned dagger in the heart of the parent State." The *Annual Register* concluded that it "is scarcely possible to conceive the degree of mortification and disappointment which the intelligence of this defeat created in Great Britain."[34]

Despite these setbacks, the press and the government still expected the war to continue until the Americans accepted British terms. The *Courier* declared that "peace with America is neither practicable nor desirable till we have wiped away this late disaster." Liverpool informed Wellington that it was still "desirable to gain a little more time before the negotiation is brought to a close." The prime minister agreed "in not relaxing further our demands after or in consequence of late events." He asked Bathurst to inform Goulburn, "we shall not be disposed to relax in the terms on which he has been already instructed we were ready to conclude peace." Liverpool expected the "continuance of the American war" even though it "will not cost us less than 10,000,000 pounds [and] We must expect, therefore to hear it said that the property tax is continued for the purpose of securing a better frontier for Canada." He warned that the war "will probably now be of some duration."[35]

The news about Plattsburgh and Baltimore caught the government in the process of again revising instructions to its commissioners. With the issue of an Indian settlement and American removal from the Great Lakes no longer on the table, Bathurst now focused on redrawing the Canadian border. Dated October 18, his instructions stated that the principle of uti possidetis was to be the basis of a peace settlement. Specifically, the British would demand eastern

Maine, Mackinac Island, and Fort Niagara. Further, if the United States would agree to return Forts Erie and Malden, then Britain would agree to return the forts at Castine and Machias in Maine. Missing now was any mention of Sackets Harbor, Lake Champlain, or any territory along the Saint Lawrence River.[36]

Since these revised terms came after news of Plattsburgh had arrived in London and were presented to the Americans at Ghent on October 21, the content of these new instructions raises the question of why the British would insist on uti possidetis after news of the defeat in New York. There are several explanations for this. First, the full implications and severity of the British defeat were not yet fully understood or appreciated. Second, the new instructions to the commissioners did not demand more American territory than the British actually held, making no mention of Lake Champlain, the Saint Lawrence River, or Sackets Harbor. Third, despite the recent news, the Liverpool government fully expected future victories. As historian Bradford Perkins has noted, "The British actually asked to negotiate on the basis not of what they held but of what, despite Prevost's catastrophe, they expected soon to hold or thought they could take." As the prime minister pointed out to Goulburn, the Americans could not mount an offensive against Canada, would continue to be strangled by the blockade, and could anticipate no assistance from Europe.[37]

In Ghent the news from Baltimore and Plattsburgh depressed the British more than it cheered the Americans. A dejected Goulburn wrote to Liverpool, "if we had either burnt Baltimore or held Plattsburg, I believe we should have had peace on the terms which you have sent to us in a month at least. As things appear to be going on in America, the result of our negotiation may be very different."[38] The Americans, however, initially foresaw no changes in the diplomatic dynamics of the situation. They had just received and rejected the latest proposal to negotiate on the basis of uti possidetis. From their perspective, the British continued to be unreasonable. "Our prospects are not more promising than they have been," noted Adams, who saw nothing that would move Britain toward a "pacific disposition toward America." Russell labeled the latest proposal as only a "new expedient for delay" until British forces occupied more American soil. Admittedly, the burning of Washington had produced sharp criticism in Europe, but Gallatin believed that the debacle in Washington had also proved "injurious to the opinion entertained of our strength and abilities."[39] Since the United States continued to be unable to defend itself, peace seemed as far away as ever.

Although the events in Baltimore and on Lake Champlain buoyed American spirits, the news did not initially convince the peace delegation that a turning point had been reached. Adams noted that the British defeat on Lake Champlain and Prevost's hasty retreat had produced "great dissatisfaction" and "complaints against Prevost" in the press. Clay observed that diplomatic events in Europe would "help us, but not so much as the events at Baltimore and on Champlain: for in our own Country, my dear Sir, at last must we conquer the peace." Gallatin and Adams agreed strongly that only more U.S. military victories produce an honorable peace. Clay thought that "we should make peace" only if British forces were beaten in the South and there were "no new disasters in the North." Adams wrote, "it is, under God, upon her [America's] native energies alone that she must rely for Peace, Union and Independence." Adams predicted, "Peace is to be obtained only as it was after the Revolution, by manifesting the determination to defend ourselves to the last extremity."[40]

It took the opinion of U.S. minister to France William Crawford to put the importance of the victories in New York into perspective. From Paris, Crawford wrote to Clay, "The naval victory on Champlain must have been as splendid and decisive in its consequences as that of the last year upon Lake Erie." Moreover, if it was indeed true that Prevost's veteran army had allowed itself to be defeated by the militia at Plattsburgh, "the prosecution of the war with a view to conquest, must be hopeless indeed." In Ghent Bayard observed that the earlier debacle at Washington had produced "great triumph and exaltation" in London and a belief that British troops were invincible. But "this error has been sadly corrected by the repulse in the attack upon Baltimore, by the destruction of their fleet on Lake Champlain, and by the retreat of Prevost from Plattsburgh."[41]

Once the ministry decided to replace Prevost in Canada with a commander who could win the war, the obvious choice was the Duke of Wellington. On November 3 the cabinet met and decided to ask him to take over in North America. Since his personal security was thought to be in jeopardy in Paris, Wellington might reasonably be sent to end the war against the United States. From Paris the duke understood that public pressure would probably demand that he go overseas, but he could not do so until the following April.[42]

On November 4 Liverpool invited Wellington to take full command in Canada. On the ninth the duke responded that he did not object to going, but he emphasized, "[I] don't promise myself much success there." Enough troops were already in Canada to defeat the Americans, whose forces "would not beat out of a field of battle the troops that went from Bordeaux last summer." Wellington explained, "That which appears to me to be wanting in America is not a general, or a general officer and troops, but a naval superiority on the Lakes." Given this situation, he did not foresee an easy victory and clearly did not want to be sent there. Instead of continuing the war, the duke explicitly advised a change in British diplomatic goals. "In regard to your present negotiations, I confess that I think you have no right, from the state of the war, to demand any concession of territory from America. . . . You have not been able to carry it [the war] into the enemy's territory . . . and have not even cleared your own territory on the point of attack. You cannot on any principle of equality in negotiation claim a cession of territory excepting in exchange for other advantages which you have in your power. . . . Then if this reasoning be true, why stipulate for the *uti possidetis?* You can get no territory; indeed, the state of your military operations, however creditable, does not entitle you to demand any." Wellington's opinion proved critical because it clarified in stark terms the formidable military challenges in North America as well as Britain's hollow pretensions for American territory.[43]

The duke's views also coincided with other developments. The news from Europe was not good. In Paris, unrest and discontent targeted the Bourbon regime of Louis XVIII. Rumors circulated that attempts would be made against the life of the French king and possibly against Wellington himself. In Vienna, the alliance that had defeated France was already under pressure. The Polish question seriously divided Castlereagh and Russian tsar Alexander; there was even private mention of the possibility of war between Britain and Russia. Since he was known to be friend of the United States, the tsar's behavior unsettled officials in London. Liverpool suggested that Castlereagh try to correct the Alexander's "prejudices," for "I fear the Emperor of Russia is half an American."[44]

In addition to the tense diplomatic situation in Vienna, political support for the war was eroding in England. British finances placed the government under increasing pressure to find peace. Liverpool now estimated that the American war would "entail upon us a prodigious expense, much more than we had any idea of." Commercial and shipping interests complained about increases in costs and insurance rates. Unpopular taxes would also have to be maintained to finance another year of war overseas. From Parliament and the press came sharp attacks on continuing the property and income taxes. "Economy & relief from taxation are not merely the War Cry of Opposition," wrote Chancellor of the Exchequer Nicholas Vansittart, "but they are the real objects to which public attention is turned." Within weeks, Vansittart observed that people had become "very indifferent . . . to the final issue of the War, provided it be not dishonorable."[45]

Then on November 18, the confidential British diplomatic note of August 19 to the American commissioners became public in London. This communication had been forwarded by the commissioners on August 20 to the Madison administration, which released it to Congress on October 10. Soon thereafter it appeared in the American press. Now this statement had made its way back across the Atlantic and was printed for the first time in London. British officials were appalled that confidential diplomatic documents would be released by the U.S. government. "Mr. Madison has acted most scandalously," complained Liverpool, but his ministry was embarrassed because the dispatches revealed publicly the demands for an Indian buffer state created from U.S. soil and for America's loss of control of the Great Lakes. In effect, the British appeared to be waging a war of conquest, a revelation that increased pressure on the Liverpool government to end the war.[46]

Meanwhile in Ghent on October 31, after the Americans had rejected the principle of uti possidetis, the British delegation asked them to present a formal counterproposal as both sides waited for London to respond to the latest American rejection of terms. Dated November 10, the American response came after almost two weeks of wrangling within the delegation. For the first time during the negotiations, the Americans had to agree on the specifics of a counterproposal rather than just concur on language to reject various British terms. On the major issues there were no differences. With the blessing of the Madison administration, the negotiators had long abandoned the end of impressment as a condition. They agreed not to accept "any other principle than that of a mutual restoration of territory" as the basis for peace. But thornier issues remained.

First was the right of Americans to fish in Canadian waters and to dry their catches on Canadian shores. Second was the right of the British to navigate the Mississippi River. Both of these privileges had been granted in the 1783 accords that ended the American Revolution. Both Adams and Clay viewed these sectional issues as precious national rights. Adams stubbornly refused to relinquish the American fishing right, one that his father had insisted be included in the 1783 treaty because of its vital importance to the maritime economy of Massachusetts. Nor did the Kentuckian Clay have any intention of allowing the British free navigation of the Mississippi. After hours of argument and haggling, the Americans finally agreed to insist on their fishing rights in Canadian waters but to remain silent on any British right to navigate the Mississippi.[47]

As usual, the commissioners referred the American position to London. Goulburn, however, did not want to compromise and was prepared to end negotiations. But once again, London overruled him. "I think we have determined," Liverpool explained to Castlereagh, "if all other points can be satisfactorily settled, not to continue the war for the purpose of obtaining or securing any acquisition of territory." Since the British now occupied very little U.S. territory after Plattsburgh, the cabinet had "been led to this determination" by the "unsatisfactory state of negotiations in Vienna, and by that of the alarming situation in the interior of France. We have also been obliged to pay serious attention to the state of our finances, and to the difficulties we shall have in continuing the property tax." A cabinet meeting on November 21 confirmed the decision.[48]

On November 26 the British conveyed their new position to the Americans at Ghent. It represented a major breakthrough for the United States. An honorable peace was now in sight because the question of redrawing the Canadian border and ceding territory to the British was off the table for the first time since the negotiations had begun. The recent military victories had been crucial. Even the perennial pessimist Adams was encouraged. "I now entertain hope that the British government is inclined to conclude the peace," he wrote to his wife, Louisa, on November 29. "We are now in sight of port. Oh! that we may reach it in safety." "The disaster at Washington was a grievous stroke upon us here, but since that Epoch there has been a flood of good news," wrote Bayard on December 6. "Nothing can be more brilliant than the victory of Macdonough on Lake Champlain nor anything more decisive in its effect."[49]

Sometimes-tense negotiations continued for four more weeks, prolonged by deliberations over the two remaining issues, navigation on the Mississippi and fishing rights. Having already conceded so much to the Americans, Goulburn did not want to compromise on the fisheries issue, but again he was overruled by London. "You must understand," Bathurst wrote on December 6, "THAT WE ARE . . . ANXIOUS . . . TO BRING THE Treaty to a conclusion. Meetings are beginning to petition against the Income Tax—& we have difficulty in keeping the Manufacturers particularly at Birmingham quiet."[50] Several face-to-face conferences failed to resolve the differences as both sides stood firm. On the fourteenth the Americans proposed that the treaty either be entirely silent on these two issues or that it refer them to future negotiations. Five days later, to the chagrin of Goulburn, Bathurst broke the deadlock by instructing his commissioners to agree to drop entirely both questions. A tentative agreement following quickly, a final treaty was signed on Christmas Eve, 1814, in Ghent. The terms ended the war simply on the basis of status quo ante bellum. Most of the issues that the commissioners had battled over for the past four and one-half months simply did not appear in the final accord.[51]

The decisive British naval defeat on Lake Champlain combined with the precipitous and humiliating retreat from Plattsburgh were pivotal in shaping the Ghent peace treaty. News of this dual disaster arrived at a critical moment to convince the Liverpool government to moderate its peace demands. First, the government still insisted on uti possidetis as the basis for peace, but it did not insert any reference to the New York border into its October 18 note since British forces no longer occupied any part of that state. Not yet appreciating the full extent of the setback, Liverpool initially assumed the war would continue in North America, where British forces would conquer and occupy additional U.S. territory. Only the combination of continued bad news from Paris and Vienna, increasing fiscal pressures, sharpened domestic opposition to the war, and a clearer picture of the military situation in North America convinced the government to moderate its peace demands and end the war as quickly as possible.

Neither the Americans nor the British were immediately pleased or satisfied with the treaty, neither side having accomplished what it initially had hoped to achieve. The Americans had won no concessions on the stated cause of the war, impressment. Nor had they secured any territory from Canada. At the same time, the British had backtracked steadily from their original position. They had abandoned their demand for an Indian buffer state or guaranteed security for their Indian allies. They had secured no territorial concession on the Canadian-American border and had failed to carry their position on the fisheries issue. Finally, the British had also abandoned their demand to gain complete control of the Great Lakes and allowed the treaty to be silent on their right to navigate the Mississippi River.

Among the U.S. delegates, Gallatin thought the treaty was "as favorable as could be expected under existing circumstances," but since "almost all treaties were unpopular," he thought this one would share that "common fate." Adams agreed with Clay that the "peace would be bad enough." The Kentuckian believed that the agreement "would break him down entirely, and we should all be subject to much reproach for it." Only Bayard disagreed. He thought the treaty to be "highly credible to us" because it "would relieve the country from . . . twenty-one millions of taxes, commerce restored, and substantially nothing given up." Although Gallatin, Clay, and Adams would later modify their opinions of the treaty, they did not leave Ghent pleased with their achievement.[52]

Generally, historians have considered the negotiations at Ghent and the resulting peace treaty to constitute an American victory. Through their tenacity and their superior diplomatic performance, the Americans had rejected and fought off a series of unacceptable British demands without terminating the negotiations. When the talks began, they were in a weak position because of the political and military situation in North America. After two years of war, the British government was determined to impose a harsh peace on the United States. With formidable military forces in North America, London expected a succession of victories in the Chesapeake and Canada. In August and September the initial news was positive for the British, and more was expected as more than 10,000 veteran troops began their invasion of New York. In retrospect, even though the importance of the events of September 11, 1814, was not appreciated fully on either side of the Atlantic, the naval battle of Lake Champlain and the British retreat from Plattsburgh represented a pivotal moment in U.S. history and the key turning point in the War of 1812.

CONCLUSION

The Treaty of Ghent was signed on Christmas Eve, 1814, sent to London, where the Prince Regent quickly ratified the agreement. On January 2, 1815, it began its journey to the United States on the ship *Favorite*, which did not reach New York City until February 11 after being diverted by bad weather on the Chesapeake Bay. From there word of peace spread quickly. On the fourteenth the treaty reached Washington. After the Senate quickly and unanimously ratified it on February 16, 1815, President Madison signed the agreement later that day. Two days later U.S. and British representatives exchanged ratifications. The war and the national crisis had finally ended.

The Battle of Lake Champlain had been instrumental in shaping the events and decisions that ended the war, a decisive military victory that came at a critical moment. Not only had Master Commandant Macdonough's warships destroyed and captured the British squadron, they had also converted an imminent British victory in Plattsburgh into a precipitous retreat. Within days, the entire 8,000-man army that had been on the verge of overwhelming American defenders in the town had hastily retreated into Canada. Planned as the major British offensive of 1814, Governor in Chief Prevost's invasion of New York had ended quickly, prematurely, and completely. It proved to be an immense and unexpected disappointment in Canada and Britain, while it furnished the United States with a much-needed and heady elixir. The fighting in the Champlain Valley was over, but the repercussions affected reputations, decisions, and events in Canada, the United States, and Europe for months to come.

Prevost's conduct produced sharp criticism, first in Canada, then in Britain. Since 1812 his plans and actions had been instrumental in defending Canada, particularly Lower Canada and Montreal, from repeated U.S. invasion attempts. He had built political support for the war among skeptical French Canadians, created militia forces, and utilized his regular forces in a skillful and effective manner. In 1814 his offensive against Lake Champlain had been planned and executed to protect Montreal from an American counterattack. Now, quickly on the heels of his defeat, both Prevost's career and reputation were destroyed. In Lower Canada the Anglophone minority denounced his humiliating military failure as well as his political conduct as governor. In London in response to criticism of Prevost from military, political, and public sources, the Liverpool government decided to remove him in what proved to be a humiliating manner. During the time required to identify a replacement, the ministry did not inform Prevost of its decision, not learning of his removal until his replacement informed him in person. Prevost's chance to explain and exonerate himself never occurred due to his death before the intended court-martial began.

In Washington the news of Lake Champlain and Plattsburgh came at a propitious moment and helped restore some of the lost credibility of the beleaguered Madison administration. The special session of Congress, which was to convene on September 19, was expected to be a fractious and angry affair since recent military news from Washington, Alexandria, Nantucket, and Maine had all been bad; more distressing news was expected from Canada. Then dramatic and unexpected good news arrived from Baltimore and northern New York. This would still be a difficult and contentious session, but the immediate military crisis had passed, even if difficult challenges remained. The nation desperately needed money and soldiers to continue fighting the war, but there were no easy ways to produce the considerable revenue and many men required. Under sharp criticism from Federalists and Republicans alike, the administration remained in disarray. The cabinet lacked a permanent secretary of war, the secretary of the treasury had resigned, and the secretary of the navy had announced that he would soon leave his position. But the reports from Lake Champlain and Baltimore served to help the federal government stabilize itself and weather the crisis of 1814.

Although the victories on Lake Champlain and at Baltimore helped end the panic in cities like Philadelphia and New York, they played the most constructive role in New England. In Boston the news helped defuse the political crisis there. During the first week of September, political discontent had reached a fever pitch in the defenseless city as Governor Strong called a special session of the legislature and local officials scrambled to meet an expected attack. Rumors circulated that Strong had secretly sought a separate peace—in fact, the governor had sent a representative to Maine discuss an armistice with Sir John Sherbrooke.[1] The British defeat on Lake Champlain and the absence of an expected attack on Boston from enemy forces in Maine diminished the intensity of the political opposition. In October the legislature easily voted to call a convention of New England states, but the political tone had changed. The Massachusetts delegation ended up being controlled by cautious and moderate Federalists, not the party's extremists. Likewise, when the Hartford Convention eventually convened in December, moderate Federalists controlled the proceedings and the recommendations that resulted from its deliberations. If Macdonough had lost on Lake Champlain and the British army had advanced deeper into New York, the possibility of a separate peace with New England would have increased and the character of the Hartford Convention would have been more strident. The composition of the state delegations would likely have included more radicals, and the subsequent tone of discussions would have been more extreme. The disaffected radicals who went to Hartford would have been in a much stronger position to increase their demands and to win much more support in the region.

Lake Champlain and Plattsburgh also played an influential role in convincing the Liverpool government to moderate its peace demands and to end the war in 1814. That September the government confidently expected word of victories in North America, intended to exact territorial and other concessions from the Americans at the Ghent negotiations, and prepared to prolong the war for another year if necessary. The initial news from Washington, Alexandria, Maine, and Nantucket was heartening. Then the news from Baltimore and Lake Champlain arrived. Baltimore could be interpreted as another British victory or at worst a temporary setback followed by a strategic retreat. But Lake Champlain could not be seen in any way other than a defeat, clearly an unexpected disaster of major proportions. Coming as a shock to the British, Macdonough's victory and Prevost's humiliating retreat fired public anger, intensified opposition to a prolonged war, and sharpened criticism of Liverpool's conduct of the war. With the deteriorating diplomatic situation in Europe and increasing domestic discontent, the political dynamics had changed. In its newest peace proposal soon after the news from Lake Champlain, Liverpool abandoned most of his territorial demands even though his government still proposed uti possidetis as the basis for peace. Then after receiving the negative analysis of the situation from the Duke of Wellington, the prime minister decided to accept status quo ante bellum as the basis for peace and to end the war in North America as soon as feasible. Liverpool wanted to be released from what Castlereagh referred to as "the millstone of an American war."[2]

Although the U.S. negotiators did not recognize it immediately, the victory at Lake Champlain and Plattsburgh greatly strengthened their position. To a man they remained pessimistic because they did not fully appreciate the importance of these events, fully expecting that it would take more American victories and more negotiations to achieve an acceptable peace. Instead, it took the U.S. minister in Paris, who was not caught up in the negotiating standoff, to place the recent victories into clear perspective. Labeling Macdonough's achievement "as splendid and decisive in its consequences" as that on Lake Erie the previous year, Crawford accurately observed that the defeat of Prevost's veteran army at Plattsburgh squashed any British hopes for a war of conquest.[3]

While the newest proposal from London presented uti possidetis as the new basis of peace, the specific territorial demands were minimal. Absent was any reference to Sackets Harbor or the northern border of New York. The American delegation now had evidence that their resolve and stubbornness combined with recent events in North America had gained traction. Weeks later they received more evidence when the British dropped their demand for eastern Maine and accepted status quo ante bellum as the basis for peace.

In addition to its political and diplomatic ramifications, the Battle of Lake Champlain embellished the U.S. Navy's burgeoning reputation and enhanced America's status as an emerging naval power. Thomas Macdonough took his rightful place in the pantheon of new American naval heroes alongside Stephen Decatur, Isaac Hull, William Bainbridge, David Porter, and Oliver Hazard Perry. On Lake Champlain Macdonough's small squadron, supported by well-drilled officers and crew, had soundly defeated a formidable British squadron. In particular, the hastily but well-built 26-gun USS *Saratoga* had outmaneuvered, outfought, and essentially destroyed the superior 37-gun HMS *Confiance*. In addition to their strategically important victories on Lake Champlain and Lake Erie, the Americans had scored stunning victories at sea during the war. To the amazement and dismay of the British, U.S. frigates had won decisive duels, while a number of smaller warships had also defeated their British counterparts. In ocean duels American warships had prevailed in thirteen of twenty-five encounters.[4] The small U.S. Navy arguably had the best warships, officers, and crews in the world. Its heavy frigates were known as the best of their class as were smaller ships such as USS *Peacock* and USS *Wasp*. Again and again, a combination of high-quality warships, audacious commanders, well-disciplined crews, and devastating gunnery had won victories over the ships of the world's dominant sea power. British newspapers bemoaned the naval results. "Our complaint is that with the bravest seamen, and the most powerful navy in the world," lamented the London *Times*, "we retire from the contest when the balance of defeat is so heavily against us." "It must, indeed, be encouraging to Mr. Madison to read the logs of his cruisers," complained the London *Morning Chronicle*. "If they fight, they are sure to conquer; if they fly, they are certain to escape."[5]

When the Treaty of Ghent reached Washington on February 14, 1815, it had been preceded several days earlier by stunning news from New Orleans. American defenders commanded by Major General Andrew Jackson had smashed a British invasion force there in early January. In the one-sided battle, the British had lost more than 2,000 killed and wounded, while the Americans had suffered seventy casualties. In the fighting the British commanding general, Edward Pakenham, had been killed.

The convergence of these events created the public illusion that the United States had won the war. An immediate political victim of the victory at New Orleans and the arrival of the peace treaty was the Federalist antiwar movement in New England. Representatives from the Hartford Convention learned of New Orleans while en route to Washington and of the peace treaty shortly after they arrived. Delegate Harrison Gray Otis predicted that news from New Orleans and the rumors of peace "will probably put the Administration upon stilts, and augur no favorable issue to our mission." When the treaty was confirmed, the Massachusetts delegation reported that its mission "has terminated ipso facto." Although the Federalists complained that Madison had achieved none of his war goals and deserved no credit for the peace, their arguments were largely ignored.[6]

The end of the war unleashed a period of national celebration. In a special message to Congress, President Madison congratulated the nation on "an event which is highly honorable to the nation, and terminates, with peculiar felicity, a campaign signalized by the most brilliant successes." Claiming no credit for himself, the president observed that the war "has been waged with a success which is the natural result of the wisdom of the legislative councils, of the patriotism of the people, of the public spirit of the militia, and of the valor of the military and naval forces of the country."[7] The *National Intelligence* claimed that the nation had achieved all of its objectives and "the administration has succeeded in asserting the principles of God and nature against the encroachments of human ambition and tyranny." The *New York National Advocate* claimed that the war had "been illustrated by more splendid achievements than the war of the revolution."[8] "From a state of humiliation in the eyes of the world," the *Philadelphia Aurora* declared, "we stand on an elevation which now commands the respect of all the world."[9]

Ironically, the way the war ended relegated the Battle of Lake Champlain to secondary historical status by the subsequent victory at New Orleans, which captured the nation's popular imagination. Andrew Jackson immediately emerged as the war's most colorful and glamorous military hero. While the nation honored and praised Macdonough, Macomb, and others, Old Hickory became the war's premier military hero, capturing the public's imagination and winning its enduring affection. Historically, Jackson's popular stature as a hero has endured. His controversial presidency notwithstanding, he remains a much better known and beloved military figure than Macdonough, Macomb, or any other figure from the War of 1812.

The end of the conflict also diminished the importance and pivotal nature of Lake Champlain and Plattsburgh in the nation's historical memory. The timing of the war's ending strongly suggested that the Battle of New Orleans had produced the honorable peace. The U.S. victory on Lake Champlain is still recognized by historians, but its pivotal importance has largely been forgotten, diminished, or ignored. History textbooks typically devote more space to General Jackson and New Orleans than to Master Commandant Macdonough and Lake Champlain or General Macomb and Plattsburgh. Other than briefly mentioning the Duke of Wellington's influential advice to the British government after the battle, most even ignore the broader ramifications that Lake Champlain and Plattsburgh had on subsequent events in Canada, the United States, London, and Ghent.

Notes

Preface

1. "Master commandant" was the formal rank used in the early-nineteenth-century U.S. Navy, although such officers were often and informally referred to as "commander."

Chapter 1

1. Jefferson to William Duane, Aug. 4, 1812, Jefferson, *Papers*, 5:293; Jefferson to Tadeusz Kosciuszko, Aug. 4, 1812, ibid., 295; Speech of Clay, Feb. 23, 1810, cited in Hickey, *War of 1812*, 68.

2. Jefferson to Duane, Aug. 4, 1812, Jefferson, *Papers*, 5:293; Speech of Johnson in Congress, quoted in H. Adams, *History of the United States*, 6:142; James Monroe to J. Russell, June 26, 1812, quoted in Hickey, *War of 1812*, 69.

3. Letter of Monroe, June 12, 1812, Monroe, *Writings*, 5:207; Clay to Thomas Bodley, Dec. 18, 1812, Clay, *Papers*, 1:842.

4. The standard American scholarly history of the war is Hickey, *War of 1812*. In addition, there are a number of other excellent histories from the British, Canadian, and American perspectives. Among them are Horsman, *War of 1812*; Latimer, *1812*; Hitsman, *Incredible War of 1812*; and Mahon, *War of 1812*. Also informative on the myths and legends of the war is Hickey, *Don't Give Up the Ship*.

5. Brock to George Prevost, July 14, 1812, Wood, *Select British Documents*, 1:352; Tompkins to Robert Macomb, July 12, 1812, New York (State), *Public Papers of Daniel D. Tompkins*, 3:26–27.

6. Cohen, *Conquered into Liberty*, 1–15.

7. Ibid., 154–232.

8. Love, *History of the U.S. Navy*, 1:13; Symonds, *Naval Institute Historical Atlas of the U.S. Navy*, 10.

9. Brant, *Madison*, 6:45.

10. Chauncey to Jones, Nov. 5, 1814, quoted in Hickey, *War of 1812*, 80.

11. Horsman, *War of 1812*, 29.

12. An excellent scholarly study of Prevost is Grodzinski, *Defender of Canada*.

13. Prince Regent's Instructions to Prevost, Oct. 22, 1811, cited in Hitsman, *Incredible War of 1812*, 41; Grodzinski, *Defender of Canada*, 70–74. A fencible was a Canadian who enlisted in the army only for home service during the duration of the war.

14. Everest, *War of 1812 in the Champlain Valley*, 53; Grodzinski, *Defender of Canada*, 76–79.

15. Williams, "Secret Corps of Observation," Dec. 11, 1886. For Williams's life, see Hanson, *Lost Prince*. Williams later claimed to have been Louis XVII of France.
16. Williams, "Secret Corps of Observation," Dec. 18, 1886.
17. Smelser, *Democratic Republic*, 236.
18. Hickey, *War of 1812*, 80–89; Horsman, *War of 1812*, 33–51.
19. Everest, *War of 1812 in the Champlain Valley*, 58–66, 87–93.
20. Hickey, "Who Were the Worst Generals?," in *Don't Give Up the Ship*, 148–49.
21. Hickey, *War of 1812*, 124–41; Horsman, *War of 1812*, 81–115.
22. Everest, *War of 1812 in the Champlain Valley*, 123–39.
23. London *Sun*, May 17, 1814, quoted in Perkins, *Castlereagh and Adams*, 38; London *Times*, Apr. 15, 1814, quoted in Latimer, *1812*, 236–37. See also Col. Henry Torrens to Maj. Gen. Sir George Murray, Apr. 14, 1814, Wellington, *Supplementary Despatches*, 9:58; Cochrane to Bathurst, July 14, 1814, quoted in Mahan, *Sea Power*, 2:330–31; and London *Times*, May 24, 1814, quoted in Hickey, *War of 1812*, 184.
24. Hitsman, *Incredible War of 1812*, 213–14, 237–38; Perkins, *Castlereagh and Adams*, 35–37.
25. Gallatin to Clay, Apr. 22, 1814, and Gallatin and Bayard to Monroe, May 6, 1814, Gallatin, *Writings*, 1:607, 612.
26. Joseph H. Nicholson to William Jones, May 20, 1814, and *Niles National Register*, Sept. 11, 1814, cited in Hickey, *War of 1812*, 183.

Chapter 2

1. Everest, *War of 1812 in the Champlain Valley*, 45–46; Everest, *Military Career of Alexander Macomb*, 54. See also Bellico, *Sails and Steam*, 205–34; and Bellico, *Chronicles of Lake Champlain*, 295–323.
2. H. Muller, "'Traitorous and Diabolical Traffic,'" 78–96.
3. Everest, *War of 1812 in the Champlain Valley*, 16.
4. Ibid., 57.
5. John Frelign to Michael Freligh, Sept. 9, 1812, quoted ibid., 62.
6. The standard biography of Macdonough is Skaggs, *Macdonough*. See also Macdonough, *Commodore Thomas Macdonough*.
7. Hanson, *Lost Prince*, 254; Skaggs, *Macdonough*, 57.
8. Eustis to Dearborn, July 9, 1812, quoted in H. Adams, *History of the United States*, 6:308.
9. *Washington (D.C.) Federal Republican and Commercial Gazette*, Nov. 25, 1812, cited in Everest, *War of 1812 in the Champlain Valley*, 90.
10. Ibid., 92, 95–96; Herkalo, *Battles at Plattsburgh*, 36–37.
11. Skaggs, *Macdonough*, 65–66.
12. Maj. George Taylor to Maj. Gen. Richard Stovin, June 3, 1813, and Macdonough to Jones, June 4, 1813, Dudley and Crawford, *Naval War of 1812*, 2:488–90, 490–91. See also Wood, *Select British Documents*, 2:221–25.
13. Jones to Macdonough, June 17, 1813, Dudley and Crawford, *Naval War of 1812*, 2:513.

14. Skaggs, *Macdonough*, 75.
15. Everest, *War of 1812 in the Champlain Valley*, 111–13.
16. Prevost to Maj. Gen. George Glasgow, July 4, 1813, Maj. Gen. Roger Hale Sheaffe to Prevost, July 25, 1815, and "Instructions for Lieutenant Colonel John Murray, British Army," July 27, 1814, Dudley and Crawford, *Naval War of 1812*, 2:513–14, 516–18.
17. Macdonough to Jones, Aug. 3, 1813, and Cmdr. Thomas Everard to Prevost, Aug. 3, 1813, ibid., 518–19. See also Wood, *Select British Documents*, 2:229–38.
18. Macdonough to Jones, Dec. 18, 28, 1813, Dudley and Crawford, *Naval War of 1812*, 2:605–606.
19. Everest, *War of 1812 in the Champlain Valley*, 125–35; Hitsman, *Incredible War of 1812*, 184–87.
20. Crisman, *Eagle*, 16; Richard K. Adams, *Vergennes, Vermont and the War of 1812*, 2; Bellico, *Sails and Steam*, 211.
21. Jones to Macdonough, Dec. 7, 1813, Dudley and Crawford, *Naval War of 1812*, 2:605.
22. Everest, *War of 1812 in the Champlain Valley*, 110.
23. Jones to Macdonough, Jan. 28, 1814, Dudley and Crawford, *Naval War of 1812*, 3:393.
24. Macdonough to Jones, Apr. 30, 1814, ibid., 429–31; Crisman, *United States Schooner* Ticonderoga, 7–10.
25. Crisman, *Eagle*, 21.
26. Grodzinski, *Defender of Canada*, 145–48; Torrens to Murray, Apr. 14, 1814, Wellington, *Supplementary Despatches*, 9:58.
27. Wellington to Bathurst, Feb. 11, 1814, Wellington, *Dispatches*, 11:525.
28. Bathurst to Prevost, June 3, 1814, printed in Hitsman, *Incredible War of 1812*, 289–90; Bathurst to Maj. Gen. Edward Barnes, May 20, 1814, Dudley and Crawford, *Naval War of 1812*, 3:72–74.
29. Wellington to Bathurst, Feb. 11, 1814, Wellington, *Dispatches*, 11:525–26.
30. Bellico, *Chronicles of Lake Champlain*, 303; Macdonough to Jones, May 13, 14, 1814; Pring to Lt. Col. William Williams, May 14, 1814, Dudley and Crawford, *Naval War of 1812*, 3:480–83.
31. Macdonough to Jones, May 29, 1814, Dudley and Crawford, *Naval War of 1812*, 3:505.
32. Jones to Madison, May 6, 1814, quoted in Crisman, *Eagle*, 29; Macdonough to Jones, June 19, 1814, Dudley and Crawford, *Naval War of 1812*, 3:507.
33. Jones to Macdonough, July 5, 1814, Dudley and Crawford, *Naval War of 1812*, 3:539; Jones to Madison, July 30, 1814, quoted in Brant, *Madison*, 6:273–74.
34. Grodzinski, *Defender of Canada*, 151–53, 159, 214.
35. Macdonough to Jones, June 29, July 9, 1814, *Naval War of 1812*, 3:537–38; Crisman, *Eagle*, 38.
36. Macdonough to Navy Department, June 8, 1814, quoted in Mahan, *Sea Power*, 2:365.

37. Crisman, *Eagle*, 34, 38.
38. Ibid., 55–63.
39. Ibid., 62–63.
40. Williams, "Secret Corps of Observation, VII and VII," *Plattsburgh Republican*, Mar. 5, 19, 1887.
41. Everest, *War of 1812 in the Champlain Valley*, 146.
42. Ibid., 153–55.
43. Fisher to Macdonough, Aug. 22, 23, 1814, and Macdonough to Fisher, Aug. 22, 1814, printed in Macdonough, *Commodore Thomas Macdonough*, 151–52.

Chapter 3

1. Horsman, *War of 1812*, 143; Smelser, *Democratic Republic*, 263; Hickey, *War of 1812*, 200.
2. Prevost to Cochrane, June 2, 1814, and "Orders of Cochrane," July 18, 1814, cited in Adams, *History of the United States*, 8:125–26; Horsman, *War of 1812*, 157.
3. Two excellent accounts are Pitch, *Burning of Washington*, and Lord, *Dawn's Early Light*.
4. Hickey, "New England's Defense Problem," 587–604.
5. Banner, *To the Hartford Convention*, 321–23; Morison, *Harrison Gray Otis*, 2:95–99; H. Adams, *History of the United States*, 8:220–23.
6. Bathurst to Prevost, Aug. 22, 1814, quoted in Bickham, *Weight of Vengeance*, 169.
7. Hitsman, *Incredible War of 1812*, 250.
8. Ibid., 252–53.
9. Prevost to Bathurst, Aug. 27, 1814, quoted in Mahan, *Sea Power*, 2:363; Izard to War Department, June 27, 1814, Izard, *Official Correspondence*, 56–57.
10. Fitz-Enz, *Final Invasion*, 91–92.
11. Izard to Armstrong July 11, Aug, 11, 1814, Armstrong to Izard, July 27, 1814, Izard, *Official Correspondence*, 54–67.
12. Prevost to Bathurst, Aug. 5, 1814, in Wood, *Select British Documents*, 3(1):346.
13. Diary of Ann Prevost, n.d., quoted in Fitz-Enz, *Final Invasion*, 100.
14. Ibid.; W. H. Robinson to Mr. Clarkson, Sept. 10, 1814, quoted in ibid., 101.
15. Grodzinski, *Defender of Canada*, 161–63.
16. "Dress Order of Adjutant General," Aug. 23, 1814, quoted in Hitsman, *Incredible War of 1812*, 254–55.
17. Williams, "Secret Corps of Observation," Mar. 5, 1887.
18. Dulles, "Extracts from the Diary of Joseph Heatly Dulles," 282–83.
19. Macomb to Secretary of War, Aug. 31, 1814, Letters Received by Secretary of War, National Archives, M221, Roll 64; W. Beaumont to his brother, Sept. 1, 1814, quoted in Everest, *War of 1812 in the Champlain Valley*, 162.
20. Williams, "Secret Corps of Observation," Mar. 26, Apr. 2, 1887; Averill, *Journal*, 4–8.

21. "General Orders," Sept. 5, 1814, *Plattsburgh Republican*, Sept. 24, 1814.

22. Williams, "Secret Corps of Observation," Mar. 19, 1887.

23. Skaggs, *Macdonough*, 123.

24. Fitz-Enz, *Final Invasion*, 94, 99.

25. Skaggs, *Macdonough*, 118; court-martial testimony of Sir James Yeo, in Wood, *Select British Documents*, 3(1):456–57; Dudley and Crawford, *Naval War of 1812*, 3:611.

26. Downie to Captain Upton, HMS *Junon*, Sept. 1, 1814, and court-martial testimony of Robert Anderson Brydon, former master, HMS *Confiance*, Wood, *Select British Documents*, 3(1):378–79, 412.

27. Prevost Proclamation, Sept. 1, 1814, quoted in Grodzinski, *Defender of Canada*, 170.

28. Everest, *War of 1812 in the Champlain Valley*, 172–73; Herkalo, *Battles of Plattsburgh*, 80–83.

29. Mooers to Tompkins, Sept. 6, 1814, quoted in Everest, *War of 1812 in the Champlain Valley*, 175; Macomb to Secretary of War, Sept. 15, 1814, Letters Received by Secretary of War, National Archives, M221, Roll 64.

30. An American myth developed and long persisted that Prevost's army at Plattsburgh was much larger than it actually was and included many more elite veterans from Wellington's army than it did. This misconception has been disproven definitively in Graves, "'Finest Army Ever to Campaign on American Soil'?" See also Everest, *War of 1812 in the Champlain Valley*, 167; and Hickey, "How Large Was the British Army (at Plattsburgh)?," in *Don't Give Up the Ship*, 76.

31. Everest, *War of 1812 in the Champlain Valley*, 176–78.

32. Herkalo, *Battles at Plattsburgh*, 96–97.

33. Mahan, *Sea Power*, 2:367–71; Skaggs, *Macdonough*, 122.

34. Fitz-Enz, *Final Invasion*, 98.

35. The term *wind* is pronounced "wynd," according to Mahan, *Sea Power*, 2:380.

36. Dulles, "Extracts from the Diary of Joseph Heatly Dulles," 276–89. For the section on Macdonough, see ibid., 278–81. Another version is quoted in Skaggs, *Macdonough*, 123–24. Russell Bellico explains that a fictionalized account of Dulles's visit appears in Macdonough, *Commodore Thomas Macdonough*, 153–56. In that work Rodney Macdonough has him dining on the *Saratoga* on September 4 rather than on August 14, which is the date that Dulles actually recorded in his diary. *Chronicles of Lake Champlain*, 305, 325n46.

37. The letters between Prevost and Downie from September 1 to 10, 1814, are printed in Wood, *Select British Documents*, 3(1):378–83.

38. Robinson to A. Merry, Sept. 22, 1814, Historical Manuscripts Commission, *Manuscripts of Earl Bathurst*, 291.

39. Prevost to Downie, Sept. 8, 1814, Wood, *Select British Documents*, 3(1):380.

40. Prevost to Downie, Sept. 10, 1814, ibid., 383.

Chapter 4

1. Lt. James Robertson's statement to the court-martial, Wood, *Select British Documents*, 3(1):471. The court-martial was held from August 18 to 21, 1815.
2. Court-martial testimony of Robert Anderson Brydon, former master, HMS *Confiance*, Wood, *Select British Documents*, 3(1):414.
3. Lt. James Robertson's statement to the court-martial, and Lieutenant Hicks to Pring, Sept. 12, 1814, ibid., 3(1):472, 495; Skaggs, *Macdonough*, 126–27.
4. The most detailed discussion is Roosevelt, *Naval War of 1812*, 2:114–26. See also Mahan, *Sea Power*, 2:371; Skaggs, *Macdonough*, 117–21; and Dunne, "Battle of Lake Champlain," 85–106.
5. Fitz-Enz, *Final Invasion*, 95–96.
6. Skaggs, *Macdonough*, 124–25.
7. Ibid., 104–105; Macdonough to J. Rodgers, [president, Board of Navy Commissioners], May 6, 1815, printed in Fitz-Enz, *Final Invasion*, 214.
8. Lavery, *Nelson's Navy*, 258.
9. James Henry Craig, *Memoirs of the Administration of the Colonial Government of Lower-Canada* (Quebec, 1818), quoted in Fitz-Enz, *Final Invasion*, 127.
10. Skaggs, *Macdonough*, 127.
11. The legend of the defiant cock is an often-cited anecdote that emerged from the battle. See, for example, Lossing, *Pictorial Field-Book of the War of 1812*, 867n1; *Niles National Register*, Oct. 1, 1814; and Macdonough, *Commodore Thomas Macdonough*, 178–79.
12. "Recollections of Hon. Julius C. Hubbell of Old Times in Chazy. Battle of Plattsburgh," *Plattsburgh Republican*, Feb. 1, 1879.
13. Robertson to Pring, Sept. 12, 1814, Wood, *Select British Documents*, 3(1):374; Bellico, *Sails and Steam*, 226.
14. Robertson to Pring, Sept. 12, 1814, Wood, *Select British Documents*, 3(1):374–75.
15. Lt. James Robertson's statement to court-martial, ibid., 471.
16. Macdonough to J. Rodgers, May 6, 1815, printed in Fitz-Enz, *Final Invasion*, 215.
17. Macdonough to Jones, Sept. 13, 1814, Dudley and Crawford, *Naval War of 1812*, 3:614.
18. Dunne, "Battle of Lake Champlain," 101; Lossing, *Pictorial Field-Book of the War of 1812*, 872.
19. Macdonough to J. Rodgers, May 6, 1815, printed in Fitz-Enz, *Final Invasion*, 214.
20. Macdonough to Jones, Sept. 13, 1814, Dudley and Crawford, *Naval War of 1812*, 3:615; "Commodore Macdonough's Autobiography," in Macdonough, *Commodore Thomas Macdonough*, 20–32, 30 (quote).
21. Macdonough, *Commodore Thomas Macdonough*, 182.
22. Macdonough to Jones, Sept. 13, 1814, in Dudley and Crawford, *Naval War of 1812*, 3:615.
23. Ibid., 615.

24. Robertson to Pring, Sept. 12, 1814, Wood, *Select British Documents*, 3(1):374.
25. Robertson to Pring, Sept. 15, 1814, and Robertson to Pring, Sept. 12, 1814, ibid., 384, 275.
26. "Recollections of Hon. Julius C. Hubbell"; R. Lea to his brother, Sept. 21, 1814, printed in Fitz-Enz, *Final Invasion*, 235.
27. Macdonough to Jones, Sept. 13, 1814, Dudley and Crawford, *Naval War of 1812*, 3:615. The British vehemently denied firing hot shot (heated solid shot) from the *Confiance*. The controversy is discussed in Fitz-Enz, *Final Invasion*, 239–41; and Hickey, "Who Used Hot Shot [in the Battle of Lake Champlain]?," in *Don't Give Up the Ship*, 133–34.
28. R. Lea to his brother, Sept. 21, 1814, printed in Fitz-Enz, *Final Invasion*, 237.
29. George Beale, Jr., purser, to Macdonough, "Return of Killed and Wounded on Board the U.S. Squadron on Lake Champlain . . . 11th of September 1814," *American State Papers, Naval Affairs*, 1: 310–11 (hereafter cited as *ASPNA*); "Return of the Killed and Wounded on Board His Majesty's Squadron . . . 11 September 1814," Wood, *Select British Documents*, 3(1):376. The U.S. total was 52 dead and 58 wounded. David Skaggs claims that Beale's list has one extra death and one extra wounding on *Saratoga. Macdonough*, 223n5.
30. Hitsman, *Incredible War of 1812*, 259.
31. Herkalo, *Battles at Plattsburgh*, 98, 116–17.
32. See, for example, Robinson to [Anthony] Merry, Sept. 22, 1814, Historical Manuscripts Commission, *Manuscripts of Earl Bathurst*, 292; and Robinson, "Expedition to Plattsburgh," 512.
33. Prevost to Bathurst, Sept. 11, 1814, Wood, *Select British Documents*, 3(1):352; Bathurst to Prevost, June 3, 1814, printed in Hitsman, *Incredible War of 1812*, 290.
34. Robinson to Merry, Sept. 22, 1814, Historical Manuscripts Commission, *Manuscripts of Earl Bathurst*, 291; Robinson, "Expedition to Plattsburg," 512.
35. Prevost to Bathurst, Sept. 22, 1814, and Cochran to Gorden, Sept. 20, 1814, Wood, *Select British Documents*, 3(1):365–66, 361–64.
36. Macomb to Secretary of War, Sept. 15, 1814, Letters Received by the Secretary of War, National Archives, M221, Roll 64; Sinclair to Baynes, Mar. 20, 1815, Wood, *Select British Documents*, 3(1):399–400; Graves, "Finest Army Ever to Campaign on American Soil?," 10. See also Macomb to Monroe, Sept. 12, 1814, Dudley and Crawford, *Naval War of 1812*, 3:609.
37. Macdonough to Jones, Sept. 11, 1814, Dudley and Crawford, *Naval War of 1812*, 3:607.
38. Bellico, *Sails and Steam*, 230.
39. Macdonough, *Commodore Thomas Macdonough*, 185.
40. Pring to Yeo, Sept. 12, 1814, Dudley and Crawford, *Naval War of 1812*, 3:612.

Chapter 5

1. Raynham deserted immediately after the battle. McGhie disappeared sometime later and did not appear at the subsequent court-martial.
2. "Memoirs of the Hon. Peter Sailly," *Plattsburgh Republican*, Apr. 6, 1872; Macdonough to Jones, Oct. 15, Nov. 10, 1814, Dudley and Crawford, *Naval War of 1812*, 3:642–44.
3. Grodzinski, *Defender of Canada*, 205–207; Everest, *War of 1812 in the Champlain Valley*, 194.
4. *Plattsburgh Republican*, Oct. 1, 1814; Skaggs, *Macdonough*, 193–95; Richards, *Memoir of Alexander Macomb*, 99–100.
5. Fitz-Enz, *Final Invasion*, 187–88. Macdonough's son was born six weeks later.
6. *Annals of Congress*, 13th Cong., 3rd sess., 386, 387. The total amount of prize money was $290,438.19 and was distributed to 379 officers and men. George Beale, Jr., pursuer, "List of Prize Money Paid by George Beale . . . October 22, 1818," *ASPNA*, 1:572–82. This total did not include the prize money paid to a few other officers such as Robert Henley.
7. Macdonough to John Rodgers, May 6, 1815, printed in Fitz-Enz, *Final Invasion*, 214; Lord, *Dawn's Early Light*, 298.
8. "The Governor's Address at the Opening of the Special Session of the Legislature," Sept. 30, 1814, New York (State), *Public Papers of Daniel D. Tompkins*, 3:536.
9. Everest, *War of 1812 in the Champlain Valley*, 163.
10. Thompson, *History of Vermont*, 2:97; Morison, *Harrison Gray Otis*, 2:107–108.
11. *National Intelligencer*, Sept. 9, 13, 1814.
12. Ibid., Sept. 20, 1814.
13. Brant, *Madison*, 6:326.
14. Jones to Alexander Dallas, Sept. 15, 1814, *New York National Advocate*, Sept. 10, 1814, and speech of Joseph Varnum, Nov. 16, 1814, quoted in Hickey, *War of 1812*, 229, 244.
15. Proclamation by Pres. James Madison, Sept. 1, 1814, Richardson, *Compilation of the Messages and Papers of the Presidents*, 2:532–33.
16. Jonathan Roberts to Matthew Roberts, Sept. 27, 1814, and William Wirt to Elizabeth Wirt, Oct. 24, 1814, quoted in Hickey, *War of 1812*, 241–42.
17. Special Message by Pres. James Madison, Sept. 17, 1814, Richardson, *Compilation of the Messages and Papers of the Presidents*, 2:535.
18. Ibid., 534, 535.
19. Ibid., 535.
20. Brant, *Madison*, 6:326.
21. Stagg, *Mr. Madison's War*, 436–53; Hickey, *War of 1812*, 249–51, 254–55.
22. Banner, *To the Hartford Convention*, 323–30; Morison, *Harrison Gray Otis*, 2:101–105; Stagg, *Mr. Madison's War*, 471–72.
23. Diary of Ann Prevost, Sept. 12, 1814, quoted in Fitz-Enz, *Final Invasion*, 178–79.

24. Wellington to Bathurst, Oct. 30, 1814, *Historical Manuscripts Commission, Manuscripts of Earl Bathurst*, 302.
25. Robinson to A. Merry, Sept. 22, 1814, ibid., 291.
26. Ibid., 292–93.
27. Prevost to Bathurst, Sept. 11, 1814, Wood, *Select British Documents*, 3(1):350–53.
28. Prevost to Bathurst, Sept. 12, 1814, printed in Fitz-Enz, *Final Invasion*, 180.
29. Prevost to Drummond, Sept. 16, 1814, Dudley and Crawford, *Naval War of 1812*, 3:616–17.
30. Bathurst to Prevost, June 3, 1814, printed in Hitsman, *Incredible War of 1812*, 289–90.
31. Prevost to Bathurst, Sept. 22, 1814, Wood, *Select British Documents*, 3(1):364–65.
32. Lt. Col. Edward Brenton to Yeo, Sept. 12, 13, 1814, Yeo to Croker, Sept. 24, 29, 1814, Pring to Yeo, Sept. 12, 17, 1814, and Robertson to Pring, Sept. 12, 15, 1814, Dudley and Crawford, *Naval War of 1812*, 3:608–14. For the correspondence between Prevost and Downie, see Wood, *Select British Documents*, 3(1):378–83.
33. Grodzinski, *Defender of Canada*, 208–14.
34. Hitsman, *Incredible War of 1812*, 265.
35. Prevost to Bathurst, Dec. 20, 1814, and Yeo to Prevost, Nov. 26, 1814, Wood, *Select British Documents*, 3(1):393–94. See also diary of Ann Prevost, [Oct. 1814], quoted in Fitz-Enz, *Final Invasion*, 188.
36. Everest, *War of 1812 in the Champlain Valley*, 199–200; Grodzinski, *Defender of Canada*, 60–62.
37. Anglican Bishop to Bathurst, June 3, 1813, quoted in Everest, *War of 1812 in the Champlain Valley*, 199.
38. Ibid., 34–35.
39. Joseph Octavius Plessis, bishop of Quebec, "Mandate for Public Prayer," Montreal *Gazette*, Nov. 17, 1812, and unsigned letter, Montreal *Le Spectateur*, Aug. 26, 1813, printed in Bowler, *War of 1812*, 66–67, 68–69.
40. Cockburn to Charles Sandys, June 28, 1814, Wood, *Select British Documents*, 3(1):336–37.
41. Cockburn to Standys, Oct. 20, 1814, ibid., 386–90.
42. Ibid. See also letter from William Dent [medical student at Montreal], Oct. 10, 1814, quoted in Fitz-Enz, *Final Invasion*, 174–75.
43. Quoted in Grodzinski, *Defender of Canada*, 215.
44. Letter, "An Englishman, September 23, 1814," *Montreal Herald*, n.d., printed in Bowler, *War of 1812*, 75–76.
45. "Extracts from Letters in a Halifax Paper," Oct. 1, 1814, in Wood, *Select British Documents*, 3(1):391, 392.
46. Grodzinski, *Defender of Canada*, 218–20; Bathurst to Wellington, Oct. 15, 1814, Historical Manuscripts Commission, *Manuscripts of Earl Bathurst*, 302.
47. Wellington to Bathurst, Oct. 30, 1814, ibid.
48. Liverpool to Wellington, Nov. 18, 1814, Wellington, *Supplementary Despatches*, 9:437.

49. Goulburn to Bathurst, Nov. 25, 1814, ibid., 453, 454.
50. Wellington to Murray, Dec. 22, 1814, Wellington, *Dispatches*, 12:224.

Chapter 6

1. Gallatin to Monroe, Aug. 20, 1814, Gallatin, *Writings*, 1:637, 639.
2. Hickey, "The Crisis of 1814," in *War of 1812*, 229–41.
3. Castlereagh to Commissioners at Ghent, July 28, 1814 (2 letters), Castlereagh, *Memoirs and Correspondence*, 10:67–73.
4. Bathurst to Ross, Sept. 6, 1814, quoted in H. Adams, *History of the United States*, 8:313; Hickey, *War of 1812*, 205. See also Bathurst to Ross, Sept. 29, 1813, quoted in H. Adams, *History of the United States*, 8:314–15.
5. London *Times*, June 2, 1814, London *Sun*, May 17, 1814, and Nathaniel Atcheson, *A Compressed View of the Points to be Discussed in Treating with the United States of America; A.D. 1814*, quoted in Perkins, *Castlereagh and Adams*, 63. For other examples of British newspapers demanding harsh terms, see H. Adams, *History of the United States*, 9:1–9.
6. Gallatin to Monroe, Aug. 20, 1814, Gallatin, *Writings*, 1:638.
7. Perkins, *Castlereagh and Adams*, 67n18; "Cabinet Memorandum, December 26, 1813," Webster, *British Diplomacy*, 126.
8. Castlereagh to Commissioners at Ghent, July 28, 1814 (2 letters), Castlereagh, *Memoirs and Correspondence*, 10:67–73.
9. Liverpool to Castlereagh, Sept. 2, 1814, Wellington, *Supplementary Dispatches*, 9:214.
10. Bemis, *John Quincy Adams and the Foundations of American Foreign Policy*, 193–94; Perkins, *Castlereagh and Adams*, 58–62.
11. Bemis, *John Quincy Adams and the Foundations of American Foreign Policy*, 189–93; Perkins, *Castlereagh and Adams*, 42–49; Dangerfield, *Era of Good Feelings*, 3–14.
12. Gallatin to Monroe, Aug. 20, 1814, Gallatin, *Writings*, 1: 637–40.
13. Bayard to Harper, Aug. 19, 1814, Bayard, *Papers*, 317–18; Clay to Monroe, Aug. 18, 1814, and Clay to Crawford, Aug. 22, 1814, Clay, *Papers*, 1:965, 971–72.
14. Adams to Crawford, Aug. 29, 1814, quoted in Perkins, *Castlereagh and Adams*, 79.
15. Monroe to Commissioners, Jan. 28, 1814, *American State Papers, Foreign Relations*, 3:701–702 (hereafter cited as *ASPFR*). For Monroe's letters to the Commissioners in 1813 and 1814, see ibid., 695–705.
16. Monroe to Commissioners, June 23, 1813, Manning, *Diplomatic Correspondence of the United States*, 1:213–15. This letter does not appear in volume 3 of *ASPFR*, which includes Monroe's instructions to the commissioners. For an explanation, see Bemis, *John Quincy Adams and the Foundations of American Foreign Policy*, 197n1. See also J. Adams, *Memoirs*, 4:51.
17. Monroe to Commissioners, June 25, 27, 1814, *ASPFR*, 3:703–705.
18. Castlereagh to Commissioners at Ghent, Aug. 14, 1814, Castlereagh, *Memoirs and Correspondence*, 10:86–91.

19. Clay to Monroe, Aug. 18, 1814, Clay, *Papers*, 1:963; J. Adams, *Memoirs*, 3:20.
20. American Commissioners to British Commissioners, Aug. 24, 1814, *ASPFR*, 3:711–12; J. Adams, *Memoirs*, 3:21.
21. Liverpool to Castlereagh, Sept. 2, 1814, and Goulborn to Bathurst, Sept. 5, 16, 1814, Wellington, *Supplementary Despatches*, 9:214, 222, 266–67.
22. Liverpool to Wellington, Sept. 2, 1814, ibid., 214.
23. Goulburn to Bathurst, Sept. 5, 16, 1814, ibid., 221, 265.
24. British Commissioners to American Commissioners, Sept. 4, 19, 1814, *ASPFR*, 3:713–15, 717–18.
25. American Commissioners to British Commissioners, Oct. 13, 1814, ibid., 723–24. News of the Indian treaty arrived on September 30. Bemis, *John Quincy Adams and the Foundations of American Foreign Policy*, 207. See also J. Adams, *Memoirs*, 3:43.
26. Bathurst to Castlereagh, Sept. 22, 1814, cited in Perkins, *Castlereagh and Adams*, 93. See also Liverpool to Castlereagh, Sept. 23, 1814, and Liverpool to Wellington, Sept. 27, 1814, Wellington, *Supplementary Dispatches* 9:279, 290.
27. Bathurst to British Commissioners, Sept. 27, 1814, Wellington, *Supplementary Despatches*, 10:138–39. See also Bathurst to British Commissioners, Oct. 18, 20, 1814, ibid., 168–70, 172.
28. London *Courier*, Sept. 29, 1814, quoted in H. Adams, *History of the United States*, 9:31; Liverpool to Castlereagh, Oct. 23, 1814, Wellington, *Supplementary Despatches*, 9:278.
29. Perkins, *Castlereagh and Adams*, 104–105, 94–95.
30. Liverpool to Bathurst, Sept. 30, 1814, Historical Manuscripts Commission, *Manuscripts of Earl Bathurst*, 294; Liverpool to Harrowby, Oct. 10, 1814, quoted in Perkins, *Castlereagh and Adams*, 98.
31. J. Adams, *Memoirs*, 3:52 (Oct. 14, 1814).
32. Clay to Crawford, Oct. 17, 1814, Clay, *Papers*, 1:98.
33. London *Sun*, Oct. 17, 1814, quoted in Perkins, *Castlereagh and Adams*, 97; Goulburn to Bathurst, Oct. 21, 1814, Wellington, *Supplementary Despatches*, 9:366.
34. London *Sun*, Oct. 19, 1814, and London *Courier*, Oct. 18, 19, 1814, quoted in Perkins, *Castlereagh and Adams*, 98, 98n35; London *Times*, Oct. 19, 1814, quoted in H. Adams, *History of the United States*, 9:35; *Annual Register, 1814*, quoted ibid., 8:112. See also Goulburn to Bathurst, Oct. 21, 1814, Wellington, *Supplementary Despatches*, 9:366.
35. London *Courier*, Oct. 25, 1814, quoted in H. Adams, *History of the United States*, 9:35; Liverpool to Wellington, Oct. 28, 1814, Wellington, *Supplementary Despatches*, 9:384; Liverpool to Bathurst, Oct. 24, 1814, Historical Manuscripts Commission, *Manuscripts of Earl Bathurst*, 302; Liverpool to Castlereagh, Oct. 28, 1814, Wellington, *Supplementary Despatches*, 9:382.
36. Bathurst to British Commissioners, Oct. 18, 1814, Castlereagh, *Memoirs and Correspondence*, 10:168–70. See also Bathurst to British Commissioners, Oct. 20, 1814, ibid., 172.

37. Perkins, *Castlereagh and Adams*, 105.
38. Goulburn to Bathurst, Oct. 21, 1814, Wellington, *Supplementary Despatches*, 9:366. See also Liverpool to Castlereagh, Oct. 21, 1814, ibid., 367; and Bathurst to Castlereagh, Oct. 21, 1814, Castlereagh, *Memoirs and Correspondence*, 9:366.
39. J. Q. Adams to A. Adams, Oct. 22, 1814, Adams Family Papers, Massachusetts Historical Society; J. Adams, *Memoirs*, 3:58–59; Russell to Monroe, Oct. 26, 1814, Papers of James Monroe, Library of Congress.
40. J. Q. Adams Diary, Oct. 28, 1814, Adams Family Papers; Clay to Monroe, Oct. 26, 1814, Clay, *Papers*, 1:995–97; Adams to Monroe, Oct. 25, 1814, Adams Family Papers; Gallatin to Monroe, Oct. 26, 1814, Gallatin, *Writings*, 1:640–43. See also Bayard to Andrew Bayard, Oct. 26, 1814, Bayard, *Papers*, 348–49.
41. Crawford to Clay, Oct. 24, 1814, Clay, *Papers*, 1:992–94; Bayard to A. Bayard, Oct. 26, 1814, Bayard, *Papers*, 348.
42. Wellington to Bathurst, Nov. 4, 1814, Historical Manuscripts Commission, *Manuscripts of Earl Bathurst*, 303.
43. Wellington to Castlereagh, Nov. 9, 1814, Wellington, *Supplementary Despatches*, 9:424–26.
44. Liverpool to Castlereagh, n.d., cited in Engelman, *Peace of Christmas Eve*, 205.
45. Liverpool to Castlereagh, Nov. 2, 1814, Wellington, *Supplementary Despatches*, 9:382; Vansittart to Castlereagh, Nov. 26, 1814, quoted in Perkins, *Castlereagh and Adams*, 99. See also Liverpool to Castlereagh, Oct. 28, Nov. 18, 1814, Wellington, *Supplementary Despatches*, 9:382–83, 438; and Hickey, *War of 1812*, 295n104, 295n107.
46. Liverpool to Wellington, Nov. 26, 1814, Wellington, *Supplementary Despatches*, 9:456.
47. American Commissioners to British Commissioners, Nov. 10, 1814, *ASPFR*, 3:733.
48. Liverpool to Castlereagh, Nov. 18, 1814, Wellington, *Supplementary Despatches*, 9:438.
49. Adams to Louisa Adams, Nov. 29, 1814, J. Adams, *Writings*, 5:220; Bayard to Harris, Dec. 6, 1814, Bayard, *Papers*, 357. See also Adams to Monroe, Nov. 1814, Adams Family Papers.
50. Bathurst to Goulburn, Dec. 6, 1814, Castlereagh, *Memoirs and Correspondence*, 10:214–17.
51. The final treaty is printed in *ASPFR*, 3:745–48.
52. Gallatin to Monroe, Dec. 25, 1814, Gallatin, *Writings*, 1:645–47; J. Adams, *Memoirs*, 3:104; Adams to Louisa Adams, Dec. 23, 1814, Jan. 3, 1815, J. Adams, *Writings*, 5:245–46, 261; Clay to Monroe, Dec. 25, 1814, Clay, *Papers*, 1:1007. See also Calvin Colton, "On His Return from Ghent," in Clay, *Works*, vol. 1, app., iv–vi.

Conclusion

1. Dangerfield, *Era of Good Feelings*, 87–88; Stagg, *Mr. Madison's War*, 472–73.
2. Castlereagh to Wellington, Jan. 2, 1815, Wellington, *Supplementary Despatches*, 9:523.
3. Crawford to Clay, Oct. 24, 1814, Clay, *Papers*, 1:992–94.
4. Smelser, *Democratic Republic*, 282–83.
5. London *Times*, Dec. 27–30, 1814, and London *Morning Chronicle*, Feb. 11, 1815, quoted in Brant, *Madison*, 6:375. For examples of British naval reaction to U.S. naval victories, see Albion to Editor, Feb. 6, 1815, and "Why Is America So Powerful at Sea?," *Naval Chronicle*, 233–34, 266.
6. Otis to Wife, Feb. 12, 1814, and Otis, Perkins, and Sullivan to Gov. C. Strong, Feb. 16, 1815, quoted in Morison, *Harrison Gray Otis*, 2:164, 195–96.
7. Richardson, *Compilation of the Messages and Papers of the Presidents*, 2:539.
8. *National Intelligencer*, Feb. 23, 1815, and *New York National Advocate*, Feb. 20, 1815, quoted in Hickey, *War of 1812*, 300–301.
9. *Philadelphia Aurora*, Feb. 20, 1815, quoted in Perkins, *Castlereagh and Adams*, 149.

Bibliography

Archival Sources

Library of Congress, Washington, D.C. The Papers of James Madison. Microfilm.
———. The Papers of James Monroe. Microfilm.
Massachusetts Historical Society, Boston. Adams Family Papers. Microfilm.
National Archives, Washington, D.C. War Department. Letters Received by the Secretary of War, M221. Microfilm.
———. Naval Records Collection. Letters Received by the Secretary of the Navy. Captains' Letters. M125. Microfilm.
———. Naval Records Collection. Letters Received by the Secretary of the Navy from Commanders. M147. Microfilm.
———. Naval Records Collection. Letters Sent by the Secretary of the Navy to Captains, M149. Microfilm.

Primary Sources

Adams, John Quincy. *Memoirs of John Quincy Adams, Comprising Portions of His Diary from 1795 to 1848*. Edited by Charles Francis Adams. 12 vols. Philadelphia, 1874–77.
———. *Writings of John Quincy Adams*. Edited by Worthington Chauncey Ford. 7 vols. New York, 1913–17.
American State Papers, Foreign Relations. 6 vols. Washington, D.C., 1832–59.
American State Papers, Military Affairs. 7 vols. Washington, D.C., 1832–61.
American State Papers, Naval Affairs. 4 vols. Washington, D.C., 1834–61.
Annals of Congress, 1812–15.
Averill, H. K., Sr. *The Journal of H. K. Averill, Sr.: An Account of the Battle of Plattsburgh and Early North Country Community*. Edited by Keith A. Herkalo. Plattsburgh, N.Y., 2001.
Bayard, James A. *The Papers of James A. Bayard, 1796–1815*. Edited by Elizabeth Donnan. Annual Report of the American Historical Association for the Year 1913. Vol. 2. Washington, D.C., 1915.
Bowler, Arthur, ed. *The War of 1812*. Toronto, 1973.
Castlereagh, Robert Stewart, Viscount. *Memoirs and Correspondence of Viscount Castlereagh, Second Marquess of Londonderry*. Edited by Charles William Vane. 12 vols. London, 1853.
Clay, Henry. *The Papers of Henry Clay*. Edited by James Hopkins and Mary Hargreaves. 11 vols. Lexington, Ky., 1959–92.
———. *The Works of Henry Clay, Comprising His Life, Correspondence, and Speeches*. Edited by Calvin Colton. 10 vols. New York, 1904.

Dudley, William S., and Crawford, Michael., eds. *The Naval War of 1812: A Documentary History*. 3 vols. Washington, 1985–2002.

Dulles, Charles W., ed. "Extracts from the Diary of Joseph Heatly Dulles." *Pennsylvania Magazine of History and Biography* 35 (1911): 276–89.

Everest, Allan S., ed. *Recollections of Clinton Country and the Battle of Plattsburgh, 1800–1840*. Plattsburgh, N.Y., 1964.

Gallatin, Albert. *The Writings of Albert Gallatin*. Edited by Henry Adams. 3 vols. Philadelphia, 1879.

Historical Manuscripts Commission. *Report on the Manuscripts of Earl Bathurst*. London, 1923.

Izard, George. *Official Correspondence with the Department of War Relative to the Military Operations of the American Army under the Command of Major General Izard on the North Frontier of the United States in the Years 1814 and 1815*. Philadelphia, 1816.

Jefferson, Thomas. *The Papers of Thomas Jefferson. Retirement Series*. Edited by J. Jefferson Looney. 9 vols. to date. Princeton, 2004–.

Manning, William R., ed. *Diplomatic Correspondence of the United States: Canadian Relations, 1784–1860*. 4 vols. Washington, 1940.

Monroe, James. *The Writings of James Monroe*. Edited by Stanislaus M. Hamilton. 7 vols. 1898–1903. Reprint, New York, 1969.

National Intelligencer, 1814.

New York (State). *Public Papers of Daniel D. Tompkins, Governor of New York, 1807–1817*. Compiled by Hugh Hastings. 3 vols. Albany, 1898–1902.

Niles Weekly Register, 1812–14.

Plattsburgh (N.Y.) Republican, 1814.

Richardson, James D., ed. *A Compilation of Messages and Papers of the Presidents, 1789–1902*. 10 vols. Washington, 1897.

Robinson, C. W. "The Expedition to Plattsburg, upon Lake Champlain, Canada, 1814." *Royal United Services Institution Journal* 61, no. 443 (August 1916): 449–522.

Tracy, Nicholas. *The Naval Chronicle: The Contemporary Record of the Royal Navy at War*. 5 vols. London, 1998.

Webster, Charles K., ed. *British Diplomacy, Select Documents, 1813–1815*. London, 1921.

Wellington, Arthur Wellesley, Duke of. *The Dispatches of Field Marshall The Duke of Wellington . . . from 1789–1818*. Compiled by J. Gurwood. 12 vols. London: John Murray, 1838.

———. *Supplementary Despatches, Correspondence, and Memoranda of Field Marshall Arthur, Duke of Wellington, K.G.* Edited by Arthur R, Wellesley, 2nd Duke of Wellington. 15 vols. London, 1862.

Williams, Eleazer. "The Secret Corps of Observation, 1812–14." *Plattsburgh (N.Y.) Republican*, December 11, 18, 1886; January 1, 15, February 5, 12, March 5, 19, 26, April 2, 1887.

Wood, William, ed. *Select British Documents of the Canadian War of 1812*. 3 vols. in 4 parts. Toronto, 1920.

Secondary Sources

Adams, Henry. *History of the United States during the Administrations of Jefferson and Madison.* 9 vols. New York, 1891–96.

Adams, Richard K. *Vergennes, Vermont, and the War of 1812.* Severna Park, Md., 1999.

Banner, James M., Jr. *To the Hartford Convention: The Federalists and the Origins of Party Politics in Massachusetts, 1789–1815.* New York, 1970.

Bellico, Russell P. *Chronicles of Lake Champlain: Journeys in War and Peace.* Fleischmanns, N.Y., 1999.

———. *Sails and Steam in the Mountains: A Maritime and Military History of Lake George and Lake Champlain.* Fleischmanns, N.Y., 1992.

Bemis, Samuel Flagg. *John Quincy Adams and the Foundations of American Foreign Policy.* New York, 1949.

Bickham, Troy. *The Weight of Vengeance: The United States, the British Empire, and the War of 1812.* New York, 2012.

Bird, Harrison. *Navies in the Mountains. The Battles on the Waters of Lake Champlain and Lake George, 1609–1814.* New York, 1962.

Bixby, George S. *Peter Sailly, 1754–1826.* Albany, 1919.

Black, Jeremy. *Fighting for America: The Struggle for Mastery in North America, 1519–1871.* Bloomington, 2011.

———. *The War of 1812 in the Age of Napoleon.* Norman, Okla., 2009.

Brant, Irving. *James Madison.* 6 vols. Indianapolis, 1941–61.

Bredenburg, Oscar. *The Battle of Plattsburgh Bay: The British Navy's View.* Plattsburgh, N.Y., 1978.

Burt, Alfred L. *The United States, Great Britain, and British North America from the Revolution to the Establishment of Peace after the War of 1812.* New York, 1961.

Cohen, Eliot A. *Conquered into Liberty: Two Centuries of Battles along the Great Warpath That Made the American War of War.* New York, 2011.

Coles, Harry L. *The War of 1812.* Chicago, 1965.

Crisman, Kevin J. *The* Eagle: *An American Brig on Lake Champlain during the War of 1812.* Shelburne, Vt., 1987.

———. *The History and Construction of the United States Schooner* Ticonderoga. Alexandria, Va., 1983.

Crockett, Walter Hill. *Vermont: The Green Mountain State.* 5 vols. New York, 1921.

Dangerfield, George. *The Era of Good Feelings.* New York, 1952.

Daughan, George C. *1812: The Navy's War.* New York, 2011.

Dunne, W. M. P. "The Battle of Lake Champlain." In *Great American Naval Battles,* edited by Jack Sweetman, 85–106. Annapolis, 1998.

Eckert, Edward K. *The Navy Department in the War of 1812.* Gainesville, 1973.

Elting, John R. *Amateurs, to Arms! A Military History of the War of 1812.* Chapel Hill, 1991.

Engelman, Fred I. *The Peace of Christmas Eve.* New York, 1962.

Everest, Allan S. *The Military Career of Alexander Macomb and Macomb at Plattsburgh, 1814.* Plattsburgh, N.Y., 1989.

——. *The War of 1812 in the Champlain Valley.* Syracuse, N.Y., 1981.

Fitz-Enz, David G. *The Final Invasion: Plattsburgh, the War of 1812's Most Decisive Battle.* New York, 2001.

Forester, C. S. *The Age of Fighting Sail: The Story of the Naval War of 1812.* New York, 1956.

Gilje, Paul A. *Free Trade and Sailors' Rights in the War of 1812.* New York, 2013.

Graves, Donald E. "'The Finest Army Ever to Campaign on American Soil'? The Organization, Strength, Composition, and Loses of British Land Forces during the Plattsburgh Campaign, September, 1814." *Journal of the War of 1812* 7 (Fall/Winter 2003): 6–13.

——. "The Redcoats Are Coming: British Troops Movements to North America in 1814." *Journal of the War of 1812* 6 (Summer 2001): 12–18.

Grodzinski, John R. *Defender of Canada: Sir George Prevost and the War of 1812.* Norman, Okla., 2013.

——. "The Final General Order Issued by Lieutenant-General Sir George Prevost, Captain General and Governor-in-Chief of British North America, 1811–1815." *War of 1812 Magazine* 11 (May 2011): 1–2.

——. "Sir George Prevost: Defender of Canada in the War of 1812." *War of 1812 Magazine* 18 (June 2012): 1–8.

——. "'To Obtain If Possible Ultimate Security to His Majesty's Possessions in America': The Plattsburgh Campaign of 1813." *War of 1812 Magazine* 3 (June 2006): 1–8.

Hanson, John H., *The Lost Prince; Facts Tending to Prove the Identity of Louis the Seventeenth of France, and the Rev. Eleazar Williams, Missionary among the Indians of North America.* New York, 1854.

Hattendorf, John B. "The Naval War of 1812 in International Perspective." *Mariner's Mirror* 99, no. 1 (2013): 5–22.

Heinrichs, Waldo H., Jr. "The Battle of Plattsburg, 1814—The Losers." *American Neptune* 21 (1961): 42–56.

Hemenway, Abby M. *The Vermont Historical Gazetteer.* 5 vols. Burlington. Vt. 1867–77.

Herkalo, Keith A. *The Battles at Plattsburgh, September 11, 1814.* Charleston, S.C., 2012.

Hickey, Donald R. *Don't Give Up the Ship: Myths of the War of 1812.* Urbana, Ill., 2006.

——. "New England's Defense Problem and the Genesis of the Hartford Convention." *New England Quarterly* 50 (December 1977): 587–604.

——. *The War of 1812: A Forgotten Conflict.* Bicentennial Edition. Urbana, Ill., 2012.

Hitsman, J. Mackay. *The Incredible War of 1812: A Military History.* 1965. Updated by Donald E. Graves. Toronto, 2000.

——. *Safeguarding Canada, 1763–1871.* Toronto, 1968.

Horsman, Reginald. *The Causes of the War of 1812.* Philadelphia, 1962.

————. "On to Canada: Manifest Destiny and the United States in the War of 1812." *Michigan Historical Review* 13 (1987): 1–24.

————. *The War of 1812.* New York, 1969.

Irwin, Ray W. *Daniel D. Tompkins, Governor of New York and Vice President of the United States.* New York, 1968.

James, William. *A Full and Correct Account of the Chief Naval Occurences of the Late War between Great Britain and the United States of America.* London, 1817.

Latimer, Jon. *1812: War with America.* Cambridge, 2007.

Lavery, David. *Nelson's Navy: The Ships, Men, and Organization, 1793–1815.* Annapolis, 1989.

Lord, Walter. *The Dawn's Early Light.* New York, 1972.

Lossing, Benson J. *The Pictorial Field-Book of the War of 1812.* New York, 1868.

Love, Robert W., Jr. *History of the U.S. Navy.* 2 vols. Harrisburg, Pa., 1992.

Macdonough, Rodney. *Life of Commodore Thomas Macdonough, U.S. Navy.* Boston, 1909.

Mahan, Alfred Thayer. *Sea Power in Its Relations to the War of 1812.* 2 vols. New York, 1904.

Mahon, John K. *The War of 1812.* Gainesville, Fla., 1972.

Morison, Samuel Eliot. *The Life and Letters of Harrison Gray Otis, Federalist, 1765–1848.* 2 vols. Boston, 1913.

Muller, Charles G. *The Proudest Day: Macdonough on Lake Champlain.* New York, 1960.

Muller, H. N., III. "'A Traitorous and Diabolical Traffic': The Commerce of the Champlain-Richelieu Corridor during the War of 1812." *Vermont History* 44 (1976): 78–96.

Myer, Jesse S. *Life and Letters of Dr. William Beaumond.* St. Louis, 1912.

Palmer, Peter. *History of Lake Champlain . . . 1609 . . . 1814.* 3d ed. Plattsburgh, N.Y., 1889.

Perkins, Bradford. *Castlereagh and Adams: England and the United States, 1812–1823.* Berkeley, Calif., 1964.

————. *Prologue to War: England and the United States, 1805–1812.* Berkeley, Calif., 1961.

Pitch, Anthony S. *The Burning of Washington: The British Invasion of 1814.* Annapolis, 1986.

Richards, George H. *Memoir of Alexander Macomb: The Major General Commanding the Army of the United States.* New York, 1833.

Roosevelt, Theodore. *The Naval War of 1812.* 2 vols. New York, 1882.

Rutland, Robert. *The Presidency of James Madison.* Lawrence, 1990.

Skaggs, David Curtis. *Thomas Macdonough: Master of Command in the Early U.S. Navy.* Annapolis, 2003.

Smelser, Marshall. *The Democratic Republic, 1801–1815.* New York, 1968.

Sprout, Harold, and Margaret Sprout. *The Rise of American Naval Power, 1776–1918.* Princeton, 1939.

Stacey, Charles P. *After Tippecanoe: Some Aspects of the War of 1812.* Toronto, 1963.

Stagg, J. C. A. *Mr. Madison's War: Politics, Diplomacy, and Warfare in the Early Republic, 1783–1830*. Princeton, 1983.

Symonds, Craig L. *The Naval Institute Historical Atlas of the U.S. Navy*. Annapolis, 1995.

Taylor, Alan. *The Civil War of 1812: American Citizens, British Subjects, Irish Rebels, & Indian Allies*. New York, 2010.

Thompson, Zadock. *History of Vermont, Natural, Civil, and Statistical*. 3 pts. Burlington, Vt., 1842.

Webster, Charles K. *The Foreign Policy of Castlereagh, 1812–15*. London, 1931.

Wood, Gordon. *Empire of Liberty: A History of the Early Republic, 1789–1815*. New York, 2009.

[Youmans, Harold, ed.]. "The Documents: 'Particulars of the Late Disastrous Affair on Lake Champlain,' [*Montreal Herald*, September 17, 1814]." *Journal of the War of 1812* 11, no. 3 (Fall 2008): 24.

Zaslow, Morris, ed. *The Defended Border: Upper Canada and the War of 1812*. Toronto, 1964.

Index

Page numbers in *italics* indicate illustrations.

111–12, 119, 126; burning of
U.S. capital as issue in, 122–
23; Canadian border as issue
in, 121–22; final treaty in, 127–
28, 129; impact of American
victories on, 121–22, 123, 126,
129, 131–33; international
events' impact on, 124;
Liverpool on terms, 119–20;
Wellington recommendations
on, 123–24
Goulburn, Henry, 109, 114, 116,
117, 118, 120, 121, 122, 126,
127
Great Lakes, as issue in peace
negotiations, 112, 116, 118,
120, 128
"Great Warpath," 10, 24
Green Mountain Boys, 11
Growler (USS), 27, 30, 92
Guerriere (HMS), 19
Gulf of Mexico, 38
gun types, in battle, 72
gunboats: advantages of, 35;
American, 39; British, 35;
British, versus *Ticonderoga*,
79, 80
gunnery errors, 81, 86

Hamilton, Alexander, 43
Hamilton, Elias, 44
Hamilton, Paul, 19
Hampton, Wade, 19, 20, 21, 31, 33,
57
Harrison, William Henry, 19, 20
Hartford Convention, 95, 99–100,
131, 133
Henley, Robert, 42, 74–75, 77, 81,
86
Hicks, William, 74, 78, 80, 86, 89
Hubbell, Julius, 77, 83
Hull, Isaac, 132
Hull, William, 17, 19, 28
*A Hundred Years Peace: The
Signature of the Treaty of
Ghent* (lithograph), 70
Hunter (USS), 27

Icicle (HMS), 79, 91
impressment, 112, 115–16, 116,
120, 125
Indian buffer state, 113, 116, 117,
118, 120, 128
Indians: intelligence gathering by,
16–17; U.S peace treaty with,
118
Inflexible (HMS), 11
intelligence. *See* military
intelligence
Isle-aux-Noix military base, 16, 29,
32, 33, 35
Isle-aux-Noix shipyard, 35, 39–41,
53, 74
Izard, George, 4, 43, 49, 51, 53

Jackson, Andrew, 133, 134
Java (HMS), 19
Jefferson, Thomas, 7
Johnson, R.M., 7
Jones, William, 5, 19, 40, 93, 96, 98
Junon (HMS), 58

King, Rufus, 5
Kingston, Canada, 10

Lacolle Mill, 34
Lake Champlain: British access to,
29; British decision to attack,
49–50; British raids on shores
of, 32–33; military presence in
1812, 26; naval control of, 35;
offensive advantages on, 50;
strategic importance of, 10, 24;
topography, 24; in War of 1812,
24. *See also* Battle of Lake
Champlain
Lake Champlain offensive: advance
to Lake Champlain, 59; army
composition in, 52; army
morale and, 52–53; casualties,
60; diversionary tactics in, 51;
elements of, 51–52; as joint
operation, 52; units in, 56
Lake Erie, 20, 46
Lake Erie squadron, 36, 49–50